# THE WESTMINSTER CONCISE HANDBOOK FOR THE BIBLE

by

C. VINCENT WILSON

THE WESTMINSTER PRESS

Philadelphia

BOOK DESIGN BY DOROTHY ALDEN SMITH

*First edition*

Published by The Westminster Press ®
Philadelphia, Pennsylvania

PRINTED IN THE UNITED STATES OF AMERICA

9 8 7 6 5 4 3 2 1

**Library of Congress Cataloging in Publication Data**

Wilson, C        Vincent, 1931–
  The Westminster concise handbook for the Bible.

"Westminster historical maps of Bible lands,
edited by G. Ernest Wright, Floyd V. Filson": p.
  Includes index.
  1. Bible—Introductions. I. Title. II. Title:
Concise handbook for the Bible.
BS475.2.W54          220.6              79–15498
ISBN 0–664–24272–3

# Contents

# Preface

IN RECENT TIMES a growing interest in Bible study has developed among lay men and women. In increasing numbers, they have begun a systematic study of God's Word.

In pursuing that task, they have turned for help to such resource materials as Bible commentaries.

Unfortunately, they often find these commentaries too extensive for their needs, providing more information than they can readily use. The result has often been one of consternation and frustration, and has pointed to the need for a brief, nontechnical guide to the study of the Bible.

THE WESTMINSTER CONCISE HANDBOOK FOR THE BIBLE was originally written as a supplement to a short Bible study course presented in a local church. The course was an overview of the whole Bible. Since that course could not, in its limited scope, provide detailed information about particular books of the Bible, the Handbook was prepared for class members to assist them in their private study.

So useful did that Handbook prove to members of the class that it was felt that such a brief guide to the Bible and its books might also be helpful to other students of the Bible. The result is this present volume.

THE WESTMINSTER CONCISE HANDBOOK FOR THE BIBLE is written for the layperson. The scholarship is not unnecessarily detailed. The size has been kept minimal, the comments brief. Included in the book is a suggestion for using the Handbook in a program of independent study.

This is not a scholarly treatise for advanced students, nor is it intended to be. It is an introductory guide for those who are beginning their pilgrimage as students of God's Word.

This guide is based on the author's own study of the Scriptures and standard reference works on the Bible. Particularly useful have been the Westminster Aids to the Study of the Scriptures, especially *The New Westminster Dictionary of the Bible,* edited by Henry Snyder Gehman; *The Westminster Study Edition of The Holy Bible;* and *The Westmin-*

*ster Historical Atlas to the Bible* (revised edition), edited by G. Ernest Wright and Floyd V. Filson. At the back of this handbook will be found the sixteen Westminster Historical Maps of Bible Lands, together with map index.

# Using the Handbook
# with the Bible

THE WESTMINSTER CONCISE HANDBOOK FOR THE BIBLE is intended to be used as a companion to the reader's own Bible.

The Handbook contains a single page of information about each book of the Bible. Each page provides background information in five separate categories:

**Author**  This section names the writer of the book (if known) and suggests other possible authors to whom the book is sometimes attributed.

**Date of Writing**  This section gives the approximate date for the writing of the book, but not necessarily the date in which the book's contents are set. Major disagreements about dates of authorship are noted.

**Purpose**  In this section is described either what is thought to be the author's intent in writing the book, or a description of the material covered by the book.

**Setting**  Under "Setting" are described the place and time in which the events of the book occur.

**Contents**  This is a brief outline of the material in the book.

A student of the Bible should approach each passage of Scripture with as much knowledge and understanding as possible. It is suggested therefore that the reader begin by acquiring some familiarity with the background of the passage at hand. The appropriate page from the Handbook will provide that information.

In addition, the reader may want to consult either the Old Testament Chronology (pages 18–19) or the New Testament Chronology (pages 63–64) in order to conceptualize the events and circumstances surrounding the period in which the passage is set. Reference to an appropriate map may also be necessary. A complete set of Biblical maps can be found at the end of this volume, together with suggestions for their use.

Bible study should always begin some few verses in advance of the passage at hand, in order that one may understand the passage in its setting.

The few minutes spent in this kind of preparation will invariably reward the reader with a more satisfactory understanding of the passage being studied.

## SOME DOS AND DON'TS IN BIBLE STUDY

### DO
- set some regular time for Bible study
- equip yourself with such helps as a Bible dictionary and a concordance
- set realistic goals
- let the Bible speak to you
- look up the background of the passage being read
- find some opportunity to share what is read
- consider using a lectionary
- become familiar with different versions

### DON'T
- make Bible-reading an endurance contest
- try to find God with the "random page" approach
- become discouraged with long lists or strange names
- begin reading with a closed mind
- use Bible study to earn divine approval
- procrastinate: read what you can today

## A BRIEF SUMMARY OF BIBLE REFERENCE RULES

A *colon* (:) always separates chapter and verse. (When no colon appears, numbers refer to chapters.)
A *comma* (,) separates single verses.
A *semicolon* (;) separates several different references.
A *hyphen* (-) connects two references and includes all between them.

## EXAMPLES OF BIBLE REFERENCES

Genesis 1–3 means chapters 1 through 3.
Genesis 1:3, 5, 7 means chapter 1, verses 3, 5, and 7.
Genesis 1:4–3:10 means chapter 1, beginning at verse 4, through and including chapter 3, verse 10.
Genesis 1:8; 2:10–13; 5 means chapter 1, verse 8; chapter 2, verses 10 through 13; and all of chapter 5.

# The Bible:
# An Introduction

GOD HAS SPOKEN. This is the message of the Bible.

God has spoken in various ways: through actual words that thundered from Sinai, through soaring poetry, through the life and history of the nation Israel. The Old Testament is the record of how God has spoken to and through persons.

The New Testament makes that Word final and perfect through Jesus Christ, the Word-made-flesh. In the life of Christ and through persons inspired by Christ, God speaks with unmistakable clarity. Whatever else may be said of the Bible, it is finally the record that God has spoken.

Because God has revealed himself through such a diversity of persons, the Bible is itself a complex document. For the Bible is not one book but a compilation of sixty-six separate books, each telling in its own way how God has spoken.

The Old Testament, for example, contains a great variety of books from many different sources: books of history (Genesis, Exodus, Joshua), a hymnbook (Psalms), Wisdom literature (Proverbs), and prophecy (Isaiah, Jeremiah, Jonah), all of which add diversity to the Old Testament message that in many and various ways God has spoken.

The New Testament is equally diverse, beginning with the Gospel narratives of Matthew, Mark, Luke, and John (with Luke's story continued through The Acts of the Apostles); extending through a great series of letters; and concluding with the majestic Revelation to John.

Understanding the Bible requires an appreciation of its diversity. In succeeding pages this Handbook will introduce each book of the Bible so that the reader may discover just how that particular book adds its voice to the great chorus of the whole Bible, proclaiming to everyone in every age that God has spoken!

## HOW THE BIBLE CAME TO BE

Just as the Bible deals with many subjects, so it comes from many sources. The stories of the earliest Biblical events (Genesis 1–11) were transmitted by oral tradition for uncounted centuries before the invention of writing. Even the accounts of Abraham (c. 1900 B.C.), the people's four hundred years in Egypt, and the exodus under Moses (c. 1290 B.C.) were first carefully preserved by word of mouth.

It is probable that sometime thereafter—perhaps by 900 B.C.—parts of the Bible, including the story of the Creation, were first put into written form, in the Hebrew language which was spoken by the people. Soon other documents were added: a history of the conquest of Canaan, the period of the Judges, and the establishment of the monarchy. Then came the message of the Prophets, the addition of the Writings, and finally the history of the nation's defeat, exile, and return to Palestine.

Naturally there were many accounts written about these later events. So varied were the manuscripts, in fact, that it was not until about A.D. 90 that the rabbinic Council of Jamnia finally decided exactly what would be included in the "canon" (official list of books) of the Old Testament, as well as how the official text would read.

The New Testament was written in Greek because that was the language most widely spoken across the world of Jesus' day (even though Jesus and his contemporaries almost certainly spoke a language closely related to Hebrew, called Aramaic). The entire New Testament was completed by the early part of the second century, but the New Testament canon was not settled until A.D. 397.

The Hebrew Old Testament and the Greek New Testament were translated into many languages. The most widely accepted Latin version was completed by Jerome in A.D. 405. The most widely accepted English version was made by a group of translators authorized by King James I of England and was published in 1611. New translations have continued to appear since that time, the most important being the Revised Standard Version of 1952.

# The Land
# of the Bible

PALESTINE is a small country the size of the state of Vermont. It is less than 150 miles long, and only 70 miles across at its widest point. The western shores are washed by the Mediterranean Sea; the eastern boundary is the line formed by the Jordan River, although sometimes the land beyond the Jordan (Transjordan) is included when speaking of Palestine.

Four separate physical sections run lengthwise through Palestine:

*The Coastal Plain.* Although the Mediterranean Sea forms the western boundary of their land, the inhabitants of Palestine were never a great seafaring people, because on the entire coast there is no natural harbor. North of Palestine lay the Phoenician cities of Tyre and Sidon, whose ships plied the Mediterranean. The people of Israel faced inland, looking toward the Jordan. In fact, Israel never quite subdued the coastal peoples, particularly the Philistines, leaving them to farm the coastal plain without real interference.

*The Hill Country.* The central belt in Palestine is mountainous; in the north is Galilee, whose mountains taper gradually from heights of nearly four thousand feet in the north to the Valley of Jezreel. This valley separates Galilee from the central mountains of the region known as Samaria in the New Testament. Among the mountains of Samaria lie the valley passes through which both tradesmen and armies have traveled for centuries. And to the south of Samaria lie the hills of Judah, crowned by its capital, Jerusalem, which sits atop Mt. Zion, 2,598 feet above the sea.

*The Jordan Valley.* From the north, small tributaries feed Lake Huleh (elevation: 7 feet above sea level), which empties into the upper Jordan. This river drops in turn into the Sea of Galilee, 685 feet below sea level, only 10½ miles farther on! The Sea of Galilee during the time of Christ supported a sizable fishing industry; it is an inland lake twelve miles long and seven miles wide. As it leaves the southern end of the Sea of Galilee, the Jordan is a clear stream; 65 miles farther south it is brown with mud, and flows at last into the Dead Sea. The latter is an extremely salty reservoir 47 miles long and 9½ miles wide that lies 1,292 feet below sea level.

*The Transjordan Plateau.* East of Palestine proper lies the Transjordan plateau, which rises into a hilly ridge just before dropping into the Jordan valley. This ridge is dissected by four small rivers, neatly dividing the region into the five areas historically occupied (from north to south) by these nations: Bashan, Gilead, Ammon, Moab, and Edom. The Israelites never completely controlled this territory, and the Transjordan is never quite considered part of Israel proper.

## THE PEOPLE OF PALESTINE

How populous was Palestine? Early census figures are not always reliable, but it has been estimated that by the time of Christ between one and one and a half million inhabitants lived west of the Jordan. The Biblical records mention 622 towns in that region, and scarcely a hilltop could be found without a village. The people were busy at many different occupations. They were farmers, fishermen, shepherds, merchants, and workers at various crafts. The industry was diverse, and the nationalities just as varied. In David's time there were still traces of the aboriginal Palestinians, as well as the Canaanite peoples who preceded Israel, and the Philistines (who probably came from Crete in the twelfth century B.C.). Later came the Greeks and the Romans. Each of these peoples contributed to the culture in some distinctive way.

## THE CLIMATE OF PALESTINE

From the snowcapped peaks of Mt. Hermon in the extreme north (elevation: 9,100 feet) to the tropical heat of the Jordan valley at the mouth of the Dead Sea, Palestine is a land of contrasting climates. In Jerusalem, January temperatures average 49° F. in January; 79° in August. But in the Jordan valley, August brings highs of 118°. Although Palestine is a dry country, barren in places, the western slopes do get rain, and in some areas farming is quite good. Still, even today the most successful farming is done by irrigation; and the possibility of famine was a perennial worry in ancient Palestine.

# The Old Testament:
# An Introduction

## THE STORY OF THE OLD TESTAMENT

The Old Testament can be briefly summarized as follows: Out of the primordial chaos, God creates the world. The human race rebels against the Creator, and God sends a great flood. Much later, around 1950 B.C., God calls Abraham to leave his homeland and go into another country to found a new nation. Abraham obeys God's call.

Around 1700 B.C., famine drives the twelve sons of Israel (i.e., Jacob, Abraham's grandson) into Egypt, with their families. Four hundred years later, the Children of Israel have multiplied greatly in number but live in near-slavery; under Moses they leave Egypt, beginning a forty-year exodus to the Land of Canaan (c. 1290–1250 B.C.). Under Joshua, the people subdue the Canaanites and form a tribal confederacy that continues for the next two centuries, ruled by local leaders called judges.

At length the twelve tribes of Israel become a monarchy and reach their political zenith under three successive kings: Saul, David, and Solomon. But upon the death of Solomon (931 B.C.), the nation is wracked by civil war. The ten tribes of the north create the Kingdom of Israel, and the two remaining tribes form the southern Kingdom of Judah.

Subsequently, Israel falls to Assyria (722 B.C.). Judah is in turn conquered by Babylonia in 586 B.C. The Temple is destroyed, Jerusalem is pillaged, and the survivors are sent into exile in Babylonia for nearly fifty years. Freed when the Persians defeat the Babylonians, the Jews set about rebuilding their homeland under Ezra and Nehemiah.

## THE MEANING OF THE OLD TESTAMENT

Viewed from one perspective, the Old Testament is just that: a testament (a contract, a covenant). From the beginning of human history, God has said to man and woman: If you will worship and obey me, I will bless you. The Old Testament is a record of God's attempt to maintain that covenant.

But starting with Adam and Eve, our ancestors vacillated, first ratifying, then rejecting that covenant. God attempted a new start through the lineage of Noah, but without success. He then sought to restore the human race through the witness of his people Israel. But Israel, too, proved unfaithful, and the Old Testament ends on a note of failure, with a world unredeemed, awaiting a Savior.

## HOW GOD HAS REVEALED HIMSELF

The Old Testament is also the record of God's revealing of himself. Through word and deed, he tells us not only who he is but also how he expects us to live in response to him. He tells us his sacred name, YAHWEH, "I AM WHO I AM" (printed as LORD in the Bible), and also his will for our lives. That will is revealed in his holy law, founded on the Ten Commandments. A history of Israel as well as an amplification of the Commandments, the first five books of the Bible (the Pentateuch) are sometimes called the books of the Law.

## THE MESSAGE OF THE PROPHETS

God has also revealed himself to us through the prophets, who were persons called to speak for God. Although God spoke directly to the patriarchs (Abraham, Isaac, and Jacob) and early prophets like Deborah, Samuel, and Nathan (the books of Joshua, Judges, Samuel, and Kings are called the Former Prophets), it is the so-called Latter Prophets through whom much of his word is delivered. These were men like Isaiah, Jeremiah, and Amos, whom God called to proclaim his judgment for the people's sins, and his promise that a remnant would be spared for deliverance.

## THE OLD TESTAMENT WRITINGS

Those Old Testament books which the Hebrews considered to belong among neither the Law nor the Prophets were called, simply, the Writings. They provide for us a rich source of insight into the mind and purposes of God. The Writings include the stories of Ruth and Esther, as well as so-called Wisdom Literature like Proverbs and Job (which wrestles with the age-old question, Why do the righteous suffer?). There are the Psalms, majestic hymns of praise and songs of sorrow; there are the accounts of Daniel, Ezra, and Nehemiah. The history of the kings is retold in the Chronicles. There is also the Song of Songs, and the gentle cynicism of Ecclesiastes. Together, the Writings add still another dimension to the complex ways through which God has spoken.

# An Introduction
# to the Chronologies

THE BIBLE may appear to be an incomprehensible jumble of names, places, and events until the reader gains some sense of the history in which these events are cast.

The student of the Bible needs a framework upon which to build in order to understand the sequence of events that combine to produce Biblical history.

The chronologies of the Old and New Testaments included in this book are intended to provide just such a framework.

The Old Testament chronology is a time-line chart. The early events from the book of Genesis (chs. 1–11) have not been included on the chart because it is impossible to date them with any degree of accuracy.

Following the death of Solomon, the nation of Israel was divided by civil war. The lines on the Old Testament chart also divide at that point; the right-hand line follows the Northern Kingdom, the left-hand line traces the Southern Kingdom. The kings (and one ruling queen) together with their dates are placed along those lines; the prophets appear in the margins at the approximate times of their ministry. The prophets have also been placed south or north, depending on the area where they prophesied.

In referring to the kings and prophets, confusion inevitably arises over the use of the name "Israel." The descendants of Israel (Jacob) were called Israelites; the twelve tribes of Israel became the nation of Israel. But following the civil war, the name Israel was appropriated by the Northern Kingdom; the Southern Kingdom became known as Judah. And Judah, under Rome, became "Judea"; its inhabitants were called "Jews."

In any chronology, there is the inevitable problem of dating persons and events when scholarly calculations disagree. Such questions are discussed within the text itself.

All dates on both chronologies are approximate, and the earlier the event, the less the certainty with which it can be dated.

# Old Testament Chronology

c. 1950–1700 B.C. Abraham, Isaac, Jacob

c. 1700–1290 B.C. Israel in Egypt

c. 1290–1250 B.C. The Exodus

c. 1250–1225 B.C. The Conquest of Canaan

c. 1225–1025 B.C. The Period of the Judges

*Samuel*    c. 1025–1010 B.C. United Kingdom: Saul

*Nathan*    c. 1010–970 B.C. United Kingdom: David

c. 970–931 B.C. United Kingdom: Solomon

## THE DIVIDED KINGDOM

JUDAH (South)                    (North) ISRAEL

931–913 B.C. Rehoboam         931–910 B.C. Jeroboam I

913–911 B.C. Abijam

911–870 B.C. Asa              910–909 B.C. Nadab

909–886 B.C. Baasha

886–885 B.C. Elah

885 B.C. Zimri

885–874 B.C. Omri

870–848 B.C. Jehoshaphat      874–853 B.C. Ahab *Elijah*

853–852 B.C. Ahaziah

848–841 B.C. Jehoram          852–841 B.C. Jehoram (Joram)

841 B.C. Ahaziah              841–814 B.C. Jehu *Elisha*

841–835 B.C. Athaliah

835–796 B.C. Joash            814–798 B.C. Jehoahaz

18

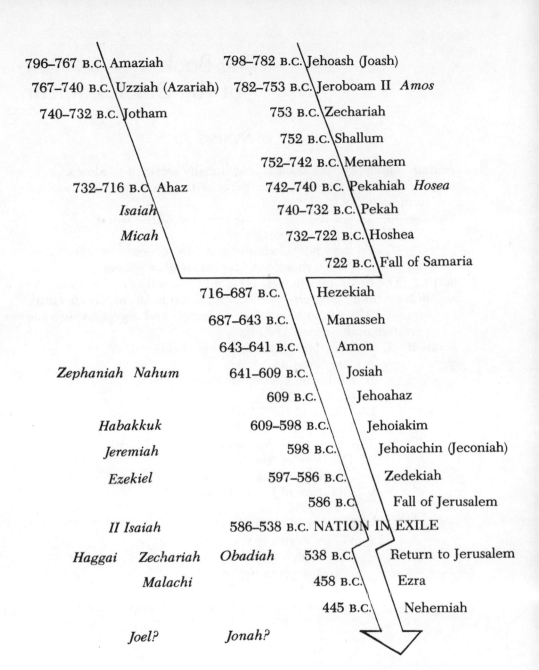

796–767 B.C. Amaziah       798–782 B.C. Jehoash (Joash)

767–740 B.C. Uzziah (Azariah)    782–753 B.C. Jeroboam II *Amos*

740–732 B.C. Jotham              753 B.C. Zechariah

                                 752 B.C. Shallum

                                 752–742 B.C. Menahem

732–716 B.C. Ahaz         742–740 B.C. Pekahiah *Hosea*

*Isaiah*                         740–732 B.C. Pekah

*Micah*                          732–722 B.C. Hoshea

                                 722 B.C. Fall of Samaria

                    716–687 B.C.    Hezekiah

                    687–643 B.C.    Manasseh

                    643–641 B.C.    Amon

*Zephaniah  Nahum*      641–609 B.C.    Josiah

                        609 B.C.    Jehoahaz

*Habakkuk*           609–598 B.C.    Jehoiakim

*Jeremiah*              598 B.C.    Jehoiachin (Jeconiah)

*Ezekiel*            597–586 B.C.    Zedekiah

                       586 B.C    Fall of Jerusalem

*II Isaiah*        586–538 B.C. NATION IN EXILE

*Haggai   Zechariah   Obadiah*   538 B.C.    Return to Jerusalem

         *Malachi*              458 B.C.    Ezra

                                 445 B.C.    Nehemiah

*Joel?*        *Jonah?*

# The Books
## of the Old Testament

### GENESIS

**Author**   Unknown; the book is traditionally ascribed to Moses.
**Date of Writing**   Unknown, but parts of the book existed in written
   form by 900 B.C.
**Purpose**   I. To tell the story of the creation of the world
      II. To explain the origin of sin
     III. To show how God attempted to redeem the human race
          first through a flood, then through a people
**Setting**   The earliest portion (1–11) is set in an unknown locale in pre-
   historic times; later chapters (12–50) begin in Ur, in Mesopotamia,
   around 1950 B.C. and move to Palestine and Egypt, where the
   narrative ends around 1700 B.C.
**Contents**   I. The beginnings of the world (1–11)
             A. The Creation
             B. Sin in the Garden of Eden
             C. Cain and Abel
             D. Noah and the Flood
             E. The tower of Babel
          II. The lives of the patriarchs of Israel (12–50)
             A. The story of Abraham
             B. The story of Isaac
             C. The story of Jacob (Israel)
                1. Early life
                2. Later life and marriages
                3. The stories of his sons:
                   a. Joseph and the coat
                   b. Joseph in Egypt
                   c. The famine
                   d. The coming of Joseph's brothers and father into
                      Egypt

# EXODUS

**Author**   Unknown; the book is traditionally ascribed to Moses.

**Date of Writing**   Parts of the book probably existed in written form by 900 B.C.

**Purpose**   I. To describe how God called his people out of Egypt and delivered them from the hand of the Egyptians
II. To tell how God gave his fundamental laws (the Ten Commandments), and to expound those laws
III. To describe how God is to be worshiped

**Setting**   Exodus begins in Egypt around 1350 B.C., some four hundred years after the ending of Genesis. The Hebrews had become a slave people, working on construction projects in the Nile delta. Under the leadership of Moses, the Hebrews began their exodus from Egypt in 1290 B.C. and continued to wander across the Sinai peninsula for forty years. Exodus ends with an account of the first year of those wanderings.

**Contents**   I. The exodus from Egypt (1–12:36)
A. The birth and early life of Moses
B. Moses' call at the burning bush
C. The confrontation with Pharaoh and the plagues
D. The Passover
II. From Egypt to Sinai (12:37–18:27)
A. The night departure from Egypt
B. Israel's deliverance at the Red Sea
C. The journey to Mt. Sinai
III. Israel at Sinai (19–40)
A. The giving of the Ten Commandments (20)
B. The Book of the Covenant and other laws
C. Public worship described
D. The people's rebellion and repentance
E. The Tabernacle constructed

# LEVITICUS

**Author**   Although traditionally ascribed to Moses, Leviticus is more probably the work of a later, unknown author.

**Date of Writing**   Part of the content of Leviticus dates from the period of the exodus and the years immediately following, but the book was probably put in its present form much later, possibly during the exile (586–538 B.C.).

**Purpose**   The Levites (sons of Levi) were the one tribe of Israel whom God called to serve as priests and keepers of the Temple. Aaron and his family were set apart to serve as priests during the exodus, and others of the Levites carried and cared for the Tabernacle and its furnishings. Later, at the Temple, they served as musicians, administrators, and judges. The whole life of the Levites revolved about the public worship of God. The book of Leviticus is therefore largely a detailed summary of laws governing both the priests and the people in their covenant relationship with God.

**Setting**   This book is a set of orderly regulations with very little historical narrative; it is a manual of religious codes describing Israel's proper approach to and relationship with a holy God. It is mostly ceremonial, but timeless ethical teachings are also included.

**Contents**   There are six main sections in Leviticus:

    I.  Laws governing sacrifice (1–7)
    II.  The consecration of the priesthood (8–10)
    III.  Laws distinguishing between clean and unclean (11–15)
    IV.  The Day of Atonement (16)
    V.  The Law of Holiness (17–26)
    VI.  Concerning religious vows (27)

# NUMBERS

**Author**   Unknown; the book is traditionally ascribed to Moses.

**Date of Writing**   Numbers is comprised of early documents and was set down in its present form around 500 B.C.

**Purpose**   To continue the narrative of the exodus across the Sinai peninsula, including the compilation of a census (hence "Numbers").

**Setting**   Numbers continues the story where Exodus concluded: the people are numbered while encamped around the Tabernacle; they march from Sinai eastward and fail in an attempted invasion of Canaan from the south; they succeed in conquering the southern Transjordan. The book ends as they are poised on the east bank of the Jordan, ready to invade the Promised Land. The events described in Numbers may be dated between 1290 and 1250 B.C.

**Contents**   I. Israel at Sinai (1–10:10)
- A. The census of the tribes
- B. The Levites and their functions described
- C. Various laws described
- D. The celebration of the Passover

   II. The journey toward the Promised Land (10:11–21:3)
- A. The complaint of the people
- B. Spies in the Land of Canaan
- C. The threatened rebellion of the people
- D. Additional laws presented

  III. The passage through Transjordan (21:4–36:13)
- A. The defeat of the Amorites
- B. Israel's encounter with Moab
- C. A second census
- D. Joshua to succeed Moses
- E. The defeat of the Midianites
- F. The setting of tribal boundaries

# DEUTERONOMY

**Author**   Unknown; to a large measure, however, the book is written as sermons delivered by Moses to the Israelites.

**Date of Writing**   The core material is old, dating from Moses' time, but the discovery of Deuteronomy (literally, "second law") in 621 B.C. by workmen repairing the Temple is one of the great stories of the Old Testament (see II Kings 22–23). In its present edited form, this second, alternate account of the giving of the law is dated around 650 B.C.

**Purpose**   As the concluding book of the five books of the Law, Deuteronomy is both a summary of how God gave the law to his people Israel and an exhortation to the people to keep the law.

**Setting**   As the Israelites are encamped across the Jordan prior to their invasion of Canaan (c. 1250 B.C.), Moses delivers three great addresses, or sermons. In them he reviews the journey from Sinai; he restates and expounds the Ten Commandments; he concludes by exhorting the people to faithfulness. Deuteronomy ends with an account of Moses' death and burial.

**Contents**   I. Moses' first sermon (1–4)
      A. A review of earlier events
      B. Victory and land as gifts from God
      C. Exhortation to serve God
    II. Moses' second sermon (5–28)
      A. The Ten Commandments repeated
      B. Elaboration on the First Commandment
      C. Obedience reemphasized
      D. The meaning of worship, feasts, tithes
      E. Necessity of national and personal morality
   III. Moses' third sermon and blessings (29–33)
   IV. Death and burial of Moses (34)

# JOSHUA

**Author**   Unknown.

**Date of Writing**   Accounts of the conquest of Canaan were transmitted through later centuries and put into this final form around 600 B.C.

**Purpose**   To tell how the Land of Canaan was conquered, and how the land was subsequently divided among the people.

**Setting**   Joshua continues the narrative suspended in Numbers, beginning around the year 1250 B.C. and ending some twenty-five years later. The story begins with the people encamped ten miles east of the Jordan; it describes their crossing of the Jordan, their invasion of the land, and the manner in which the territory was divided.

**Contents**   I. The conquest of Canaan (1–12)
    A. Joshua as commander of Israel
    B. The crossing of the Jordan
    C. The fall of Jericho
    D. The sin of Achan; failure, then victory at Ai
    E. The southern campaign
    F. The northern campaign
II. Israel's tribes are assigned territories (13–21). NOTE: Tribe of Levi (priests) is assigned Cities of Refuge.
    A. Reuben
    B. Gad
    C. Manasseh (half-tribe, from Joseph)
    D. Judah
    E. Ephraim (half-tribe, from Joseph)
    F. Benjamin
    G. Simeon
    H. Zebulun
    I. Issachar
    J. Asher
    K. Naphtali
    L. Dan
III. Joshua's farewell and death (22–24)

# JUDGES

**Author**   Unknown.

**Date of Writing**   Almost certainly these stories were put into writing long before the book reached its present form (around 600 B.C.). The song of Deborah, for example, dates from around 1100 B.C. and has an eyewitness quality about it.

**Purpose**   I. To describe how Israel lived and grew in the two centuries following the conquest of Canaan, a time when everyone did "what was right in his own eyes"

II. To show that victory came from God, while idolatry always wrought disaster

**Setting**   Judges covers the years in Israel's history between 1225 and 1025 B.C. It was a period when the twelve tribes formed a loosely knit confederation without central power or real unity. Justice was administered by local officers called judges. This same term was also applied to the leaders whom God raised up to guide the people in battle during these years.

**Contents**   I. Preface (1:1–2:5)

II. Stories of the judges (2:6–16:31)

A. Othniel

B. Ehud and Shamgar

C. Deborah and Barak

D. Gideon

E. Abimelech (not a judge)

F. Tola and Jair

G. Jephthah

H. Ibzan, Elon, Abdon

I. Samson

III. Chaos and moral decay in Israel (17–21)

# RUTH

**Author**  Unknown.

**Date of Writing**  Uncertain, but probably relatively late, possibly between 550 and 450 B.C., or even as late as 350 B.C. The date must be postexilic, since the procedure advocated in Deuteronomy 25:9 seems already obsolete and in need of explanation (Ruth 4:7). Although it stands between Judges and Samuel in the English Bible, The Book of Ruth is not among the "Former Prophets"; in the Hebrew Bible it is included among the Writings.

**Purpose**  The writer possibly intends the book as a lesson against the narrow exclusiveness advocated by Ezra and Nehemiah in regard to foreign marriages; certainly the writer intends this story to be a lesson in faithfulness and its reward.

**Setting**  The story takes place in Moab and Judah during the period of the Judges, around 1150 B.C. Ruth is the great-grandmother of King David.

**Contents**  I. Ruth widowed in Moab
II. The return of Ruth and Naomi to Bethlehem
III. Ruth befriended by Boaz, a kinsman
IV. The marriage of Ruth and Boaz

# I SAMUEL

**Author**   Unknown. The name of Samuel is given to the book because he is the first great figure dealt with in I Samuel.

**Date of Writing**   The two books of Samuel were originally a single book, which, woven together from a variety of sources, was completed in its present form by 600 B.C.

**Purpose**   I. To describe the events in the life of Israel during the years between 1070 and 1010 B.C.

      II. To trace the life stories of Samuel, Saul, and David

     III. To show how Israel's sins brought defeat, and how faithfulness led to victory

**Setting**   I Samuel begins with the final years of the Judges, around 1070 B.C. It subsequently describes the birth and life of Samuel, the last of the judges; Samuel's anointing of Saul; and the subsequent choice of David to be king. I Samuel ends with the death of Saul, 1010 B.C.

**Contents**   I. The life of Samuel (1–10:16)

      A. The birth and early life of Samuel

      B. The war with the Philistines

      C. Samuel as judge

      D. Saul chosen by Samuel

    II. The kingdom under Saul (10:17–31:13)

      A. Saul as the first king

      B. Saul's failure in crisis

      C. David secretly chosen to succeed Saul

      D. Israel delivered from the Philistines by David

      E. Saul's turning on David

      F. David as outlaw

      G. David's service with the Philistines

      H. Defeat of the Amalekites by David

      I. Death of Saul

# II SAMUEL

**Author**  Unknown. The name of Samuel is given because he is the first great figure dealt with in I Samuel.

**Date of Writing**  The two books of Samuel were originally a single book, which, woven together from a variety of sources, was completed in its present form by 600 B.C.

**Purpose**  I. To describe the events in the life of Israel during the years between 1010 and 970 B.C.

II. To complete the story of the life of David

III. To show how Israel's sins brought defeat, and how faithfulness led to victory

**Setting**  II Samuel begins with the death of Saul in 1010 B.C., traces the life of David with all its successes and failures, and concludes just before David's death in 970 B.C.

**Contents**  I. David as king in Hebron (1–4)

A. David anointed king of Judah at Hebron

B. Civil war

II. David as king of all Israel (5–24)

A. The establishment of Jerusalem as national capital

B. The kingdom extended by David

C. David and Bathsheba

D. Amnon, Tamar, and Absalom

E. The revolt of Absalom

F. The defeat and death of Absalom

G. The return of David to Jerusalem

H. Later events in David's reign

# I KINGS

**Author**  Unknown.

**Date of Writing**  I and II Kings were originally one book, compiled as a history of the kings of Israel and Judah by an unknown editor from the Southern Kingdom between 600 and 550 B.C. For his sources, the writer drew on court annals from both kingdoms; a chronicle of the activities of the Temple kept from Solomon's time; and word-of-mouth stories of the prophets and kings whose lives are here recorded

**Purpose**  I. To preserve a record of the monarchy from the time of Solomon to the death of Ahab

  II. To show how the good kings were those faithful to the commandments of God

  III. To describe God's judgment on a sinful nation, as that judgment was pronounced by the prophets

**Setting**  I Kings begins with David's death and Solomon's accession to the throne (970 B.C.). It continues through the reign of Solomon and the civil war that followed his death, ending with the death of Ahab in 853 B.C.

**Contents**  I. The reign of Solomon (1–11)

  A. A contest for the throne

  B. Solomon anointed king

  C. The building of the Temple

  D. The extension of the kingdom

  E. The visit of the Queen of Sheba

  F. Growing dissension

  G. Death of Solomon; succession of Rehoboam

  II. The kingdom divided (12–22)

  A. The separation of Judah and Israel

  B. Baal worship established in Israel

  C. Elijah, Ahab, and Jezebel

  D. Naboth's vineyard and the death of Ahab

# II KINGS

**Author**   Unknown.

**Date of Writing**   I and II Kings were originally one book, compiled as a history of the kings of Israel and Judah. The unknown editor, sometime between 600 and 550 B.C., wove together material gathered from varied sources.

**Purpose**   I. To preserve a record of the monarchy from the death of Ahab (853 B.C.) to the fall of Jerusalem (586 B.C.)

II. To show how the good kings were those faithful to the commandments of God

III. To describe God's judgment on a sinful nation, as that judgment was pronounced by the prophets

**Setting**   II Kings picks up the story of the kings and the prophets in 853 B.C. and traces the subsequent history of the next two and a half centuries, ending with the fall of Jerusalem, 586 B.C.

**Contents**   I. The alliance of North and South (1–8)
- A. Elijah succeeded by Elisha
- B. Jehoram and Jehoshaphat united in war
- C. The story of Naaman the leper
- D. The revolt of Edom against Judah

II. The separation of North and South (9–15:7)
- A. The revolt of Jehu
- B. The suppression of Baal worship in Israel
- C. Continuing war with Syria
- D. Resumption of war between North and South
- E. The following half century of peace

III. The conquest of Israel by Assyria (15:8–17:41)

IV. The last days of Judah (18–25)
- A. The deliverance of Jerusalem from Assyria
- B. Idolatry prevails in Judah
- C. Reforms of Josiah
- D. The siege and fall of Jerusalem
- E. The exile to Babylonia

# I CHRONICLES

**Author**   An unknown writer often referred to as "the Chronicler."

**Date of Writing**   Between 350 and 300 B.C. Originally, I and II Chronicles, Ezra, and Nehemiah were one book. The Chronicler, writing long after the exile, knew and used the books of Samuel and Kings.

**Purpose**   Just as the editor or editors of Samuel and Kings were concerned primarily with the morality and the activities of the kings of Israel and Judah, the Chronicler is concerned with priestly things: the worship in the Temple, the transfer of the Ark, the building of the altar. The first purpose of the writer is thus to present the correct procedure for the worship of God. His second purpose is to show that the plan of God is to be fulfilled through the Southern Kingdom, Judah.

**Setting**   Following nine chapters of genealogies, I Chronicles gives a history of the Israelites from Adam until the death of David in 970 B.C.

**Contents**   I. The lineage of the chosen people (1–9)
  II. The reign of David (10–29)
    A. Saul dies and is succeeded by David
    B. The establishment of David's kingdom
    C. The moving of the Ark during the Philistine wars
    D. David's conquests enumerated
    E. Preparations for building the Temple
    F. David succeeded by Solomon

# II CHRONICLES

**Author**   The Chronicler (see I Chronicles, "Author").

**Date of Writing**   Between 350 and 300 B.C. Originally, I and II Chronicles, Ezra, and Nehemiah were one book. The Chronicler, writing long after the exile, knew and used the books of Samuel and Kings.

**Purpose**   Just as the editor or editors of Samuel and Kings were concerned primarily with the morality and the activities of the kings of Israel and Judah, the Chronicler is concerned with priestly things: the worship in the Temple, the transfer of the Ark, the building of the altar. The first purpose of the writer is thus to present the correct procedure for the worship of God. His second purpose is to show that the plan of God is to be fulfilled through the Southern Kingdom, Judah.

**Setting**   II Chronicles begins with the reign of Solomon (970 B.C.) and ends with the edict of Cyrus of Persia to permit the exiles to return home from Babylon (538 B.C.).

**Contents**   I. The reign of Solomon (1–9)
      A. The building of the Temple
      B. The dedication of the Temple
      C. Later events in Solomon's life
   II. The kingdom divided (10–36)
      A. Jeroboam and Rehoboam
      B. Asa: a God-fearing king
      C. Jehoshaphat's reign
      D. The Temple repaired by Joash
      E. The reforms of Hezekiah
      F. Jerusalem spared from the Assyrians
      G. The idolatry of Judah
      H. The reforms of Josiah
      I. The fall of Jerusalem; the exile

# EZRA

**Author**  The Chronicler (see I Chronicles, "Author").

**Date of Writing**  Between 350 and 300 B.C.

**Purpose**  I. To continue the Chronicler's interpretation of Jewish history during the century after the exile

II. To show that success during the period came with renewed obedience to the law of God, particularly in practices of worship

**Setting**  The land of Judah, between 538 and 432 B.C. The books of Ezra and Nehemiah were originally one book. After describing the first return in 538, and subsequent events, these books tell how the two leaders returned to Jerusalem and initiated both religious reform and substantial rebuilding within the city. Ezra the scribe returned to Jerusalem in 458 B.C.; Nehemiah the governor returned first in 445, then again in 432.

**Contents**  I. The return to Jerusalem (1–6)
   A. Lists of returning exiles
   B. Foundations laid for a new Temple
   C. An interruption of the work
   D. The completion of the Temple
II. The return of Ezra to Jerusalem (7–10)
   A. Ezra authorized to begin religious reform
   B. Foreign marriages condemned

# NEHEMIAH

**Author**  The Chronicler (see I Chronicles, "Author").

**Date of Writing**  Between 350 and 300 B.C.

**Purpose**  I. To continue the Chronicler's interpretation of Jewish history during the century after the exile

II. To show that success during the period came with renewed obedience to the law of God, particularly in practices of worship

**Setting**  The land of Judah, between 538 and 432 B.C. The books of Ezra and Nehemiah were originally one book. After describing the first return in 538, and subsequent events, these books tell how the two leaders returned to Jerusalem and initiated both religious reform and substantial rebuilding within the city. Ezra the scribe returned to Jerusalem in 458 B.C.; Nehemiah the governor returned first in 445, then again in 432.

**Contents**  I. Nehemiah's return to Jerusalem (1–7)
   A. A description of his appointment
   B. Nehemiah's return and the start of rebuilding
   C. The walls rebuilt
   D. Economic reform introduced
   E. A list of returning exiles

II. Ezra's reading of the Law (8–10)
   A. The Law presented to the assembled people
   B. The people's response in repentance
   C. The renewal of the covenant

III. Official census lists (11:1–13:3)

IV. Nehemiah's second visit to Jerusalem, bringing reforms (13:4–31)

# ESTHER

**Author**  Unknown.

**Date of Writing**  Probably around 250 B.C.

**Purpose**  To explain the origin of the Feast of Purim, which commemorates the victory of the Jews over their enemies.

**Setting**  The story of Esther takes place at about the time of Ezra (around 470 B.C.), when the Persian empire was supreme, and its king was Xerxes I (called Ahasuerus in Esther). Susa was a capital city of the Persian empire, the king's winter residence, and this is the locale of the story.

**Contents**  I.  The disaffection of the Persian king for his queen, and her banishment
 II.  The selection of a Jew, Esther, to be queen
 III.  The king's life saved by Esther's guardian, Mordecai
 IV.  Mordecai's refusal to obey the chief prince Haman
 V.  Haman's plot for revenge: the execution of all Jews
 VI.  The intervention of Mordecai and Esther
 VII.  The deliverance of the Jews, and the slaying of their enemies
 VIII.  The Feast of Purim established

# JOB

**Author**   Unknown.

**Date of Writing**   Not known with any certainty. Its language and literary style indicate that the present book was written between 600 and 300 B.C. But the original story comes from a much earlier era. From Ezekiel 14:14–20 we know that Job was regarded as an ancient figure of righteousness.

**Purpose**   To raise, and answer, the question: Why do the righteous suffer?

**Setting**   Ch. 1 begins on a day long, long ago, when God was challenged by Satan to test the faith of a very righteous man named Job. Job's home was in the land of Uz, the location of which we cannot definitely place. The test is repeated and intensified in ch. 2. The rest of the book is poetic, a stylized dialogue between Job, his friends, and God—returning to prose to conclude the story at the very end of ch. 42.

**Contents**   I. The test (1–2)
- A. Job's faithfulness to God even after losing his fortune and family
- B. Job's faithfulness when afflicted with physical pain

    II. The arguments about suffering, its cause and its meaning (3:1–42:6)
- A. The argument of three friends (Eliphaz, Bildad, Zophar) that Job's pain must be punishment
- B. Job's denial of wrongdoing and questioning of his suffering
- C. Job reminded by God (first through Elihu, then directly) of his limited knowledge of God's will
- D. Job's affirmation that God must be trusted

    III. Job's fortunes restored (42:7–17)

# PSALMS

**Author**   The book is traditionally ascribed to David, who may indeed have composed a part of The Psalms. But the authors of most of the psalms are unknown.

**Date of Writing**   Some portions date from the time of David, c. 1000 B.C., particularly Psalms 3 through 41, which were the first to be gathered as a group to form a psalter. The 150 psalms represent five different collections that were finally assembled as The Book of Psalms (the Psalter) by 300 B.C.

**Purpose**   While the first psalms seem to have been hymns designed for worship in the Temple, other types of psalms gradually were added: private devotional psalms, psalms of lament, psalms of national historical celebration. The purpose of the whole collection seems to be to provide a variety of aids to worship, much as modern hymnals are constructed.

**Setting**   There is no single setting for the psalms; the tone and content of each psalm must be considered separately.

**Contents**   Psalms is divided into five collections, or books:

Book I      Psalms 1–41
Book II     Psalms 42–72
Book III    Psalms 73–89
Book IV     Psalms 90–106
Book V      Psalms 107–150

Each of these books ends with a doxology, while the final psalm (150) is a doxology marking the end both of Book V and of the whole Psalter.

# PROVERBS

**Author**  Many of the proverbs are attributed to Solomon, but the authorship is difficult to establish; nothing is known of Agur (30:1) or Lemuel (31:1).

**Date of Writing**  The present book is a compilation of seven different collections of proverbs, drawn from different periods in Israel's history. Some of the collections are considerably older than others. Any proverb written by Solomon would have been composed by 931 B.C., while the book itself came into its present form around 350 B.C.

**Purpose**  To provide instruction in practical matters of living.

**Setting**  Proverbs is classified as Wisdom literature. The sayings may have been used in formal learning situations, but they found ready acceptance among the common people. They were transmitted from parent to child, from scholar to scholar, from Temple to home, and from friend to friend. Whatever their sources, the proverbs were gradually refined and sharpened, and compiled into the present collection.

**Contents**  Proverbs combines the following seven collections:
   I. Chs. 1:1–9:18 (attributed to Solomon)
  II. Chs. 10:1–22:16 (attributed to Solomon)
 III. Chs. 22:17–24:34
  IV. Chs. 25:1–29:27 (attributed to Solomon)
   V. Ch. 30:1–33 (attributed to Agur)
  VI. Ch. 31:1–9 (attributed to Lemuel)
 VII. Ch. 31:10–31

# ECCLESIASTES

**Author**   Unknown. The author is almost certainly not Solomon, "the son of David" (1:1). The name Ecclesiastes refers to one who speaks in an assembly, a preacher or teacher.

**Date of Writing**   Very late, possibly around 200 B.C.

**Purpose**   Writing in discouraging times, the Preacher speaks of the futility of life. "Vanity of vanities, all is vanity" is the theme of Ecclesiastes. Ecclesiastes is a piece of Jewish Wisdom literature.

**Setting**   After the exile the Temple has been rebuilt and sacrifice and other forms of worship have been restored, but conditions have not improved. In this context the writer is pessimistic. Altogether, this is a compilation of thirty or forty maxims on the general subject of the Preacher's inability to find meaning in life.

**Contents**   There is no formal plan to the book, but the subjects covered are:

     I.  The vanity of human life (1:1–11)
    II.  The search for meaning in life (1:12–2:26)
   III.  The times for all things (3:1–9)
   IV.  The unfairness of life (3:10–5:7)
    V.  The futility of labor (5:8–6:12)
   VI.  Comments about wisdom (7:1–8:13; 10:1–11:10)
  VII.  The certainty of death (8:14–9:18; 12:1–8)
 VIII.  Man's duty to fear and obey God (12:9–14)

# SONG OF SOLOMON

**Author**   The book is ascribed to Solomon, but other than the title there is no evidence that he was the author.

**Date of Writing**   Linguists, noting the style and the form of the language, place the date of writing after the exile, perhaps as late as 300 B.C. The author possibly used material from an earlier period. The book is also known as The Song of Songs.

**Purpose**   Various interpretations have been given for this writing. It has been called an allegory of God's love for Israel; a Christian message of the love of Christ for the church; even a pagan liturgy. But it is most probably exactly what it seems: a love poem that had been considered allegorical for so long that by the time the canon was completed, this book was included.

**Setting**   This poem has no particular setting. Its message is both timeless and universal. It soars with unstructured expressions of love, and has no formal plot.

**Contents**   One possible interpretation of the book is set forth in the following outline:

    I. The complaint of the Shulamite maiden (1:2–7)
    II. Solomon's attempt to win her love (1:8–2:7)
    III. The memory of her shepherd-lover (2:8–17)
    IV. A recent dream of her lover (3:1–5)
    V. Solomon's continued attempt to win her (3:6–11)
    VI. Solomon's persistence (4:1–8)
    VII. An idealized discourse between maiden and lover (4:9–5:1)
    VIII. The maiden's second dream (5:2–8)
    IX. Surprise is expressed at her rejection of the king (5:9–6:3)
    X. Another attempt to win her love (6:4–13)
    XI. The final attempt of the king (7:1–9)
    XII. Her restatement of love for the shepherd (7:10–8:4)
    XIII. The maiden and the shepherd are reunited (8:5–14)

# ISAIAH

**Author**   The Book of Isaiah, the first of the three Major Prophets, has been traditionally ascribed to the prophet of that name. Isaiah is probably the author of most of chs. 1–39. Chs. 40–55 belong to a different time and probably a different author, sometimes called Second Isaiah. Chs. 56–66 seem to be from still a third source.

**Date of Writing**   Chs. 1–39 date from the time of Isaiah, who was called to be a prophet (6:1) in the year that King Uzziah died (740 B.C.). Chs. 40–55 were likely written just before the Jews returned to Palestine (perhaps in 540 B.C.). Chs. 56–66 are still later (between 520 and 450 B.C.).

**Purpose**   The message of chs. 1–39 is a prophecy of judgment and defeat unless the nation repents, a warning that only a faithful remnant will be spared. Second Isaiah, following the destruction of Jerusalem and the deportation of the Jews to Babylon, announces that God is coming to restore the nation; that its suffering has been for the sins of the world. Chs. 56–66 speak of a new and more glorious tomorrow for the faithful.

**Setting**   Chs. 1–39 are set in Judah; chs. 40–55 have their locale in Babylon; chs. 56–66 are from Jerusalem.

**Contents**   I. Prophecies of judgment (1–39)
- A. A call to repentance in the face of doom
- B. The call of Isaiah
- C. God, not Assyria, to save Judah
- D. Judgment on the nations of the world
- E. The coming Day of the Lord
- F. Failure of the Assyrian invasion

II. God to restore his people (40–55)
- A. God to take his people home
- B. Israel as the Servant of the Lord
- C. The Servant's sufferings explained

III. The need for repentance in restoration (56–66)

# JEREMIAH

**Author**  Jeremiah, the second Major Prophet. Certain additional material has been included in the book.

**Date of Writing**  The prophecies were delivered between 626 and 586 B.C., and these appear in the first person. Biographical and historical material written in the third person was added later from other sources. Jeremiah's scribe Baruch is the probable source of much of this material.

**Purpose**  To proclaim that God would bring a terrible judgment on the people for their sins by an instrument he would raise up (Nebuchadnezzar), but that following this disaster there would come a day of redemption.

**Setting**  The book is set in Judah during the forty years prior to the fall of Jerusalem in 586 B.C. Unfortunately, various parts of Jeremiah are out of chronological order; as it stands, the book is divided into five sections, as outlined below.

**Contents**
I. Jeremiah's call and early visions (1)
II. Prophecies against Judah (2–25)
    A. Judah's sins enumerated
    B. Disaster impending
    C. False and sterile worship condemned
    D. Insincere reforms condemned
    E. The parable of the potter
    F. The promise of a messiah-king
III. An account of Jeremiah's ministry (26–45)
    A. Various prophecies
    B. Restoration is promised
    C. Other historical data
IV. Additional prophecies against the nations (46–51)
V. The destruction of Jerusalem (52)

# LAMENTATIONS

**Author** Traditionally ascribed to Jeremiah, this book is probably the work of an unknown author or authors.

**Date of Writing** Chs. 2 and 4 were probably written by eyewitnesses to the fall of Jerusalem (586 B.C.), while chs. 1 and 3 seem to have been inspired by The Book of Jeremiah. The date of the composition of Lamentations as a book is unknown.

**Purpose** Lamentations is an outpouring of grief over a fallen city, ending with a prayer for restoration.

**Setting** The book is set in Jerusalem just after the city was totally destroyed by the Babylonians in 586 B.C.

**Contents** Only five chapters long, Lamentations may be outlined as follows:

    I. The desolation of fallen Jerusalem (1)
    II. The judgment of the Lord (2)
    III. The hope for the future (3)
    IV. The justification for punishment (4)
    V. A prayer for restoration (5)

# EZEKIEL

**Author**   The third Major Prophet, Ezekiel. The book includes later editorial additions.

**Date of Writing**   Ezekiel was a contemporary of Jeremiah; he was a priest in Jerusalem, carried away during Nebuchadnezzar's first invasion (597 B.C.). His prophetic career began about 593 B.C., and his last prophecies date from 573 B.C.

**Purpose**   Ezekiel proclaims that the judgment of God has come and will come upon the people for their sins. But he also foresees that a faithful remnant will be restored to their land.

**Setting**   Ezekiel's call can be dated in the year 593 B.C., and the prophecies continue through the fall of Jerusalem until his final visions (in 573 B.C.) of a new Jerusalem. When the book opens, Ezekiel has already been carried into captivity by the first Babylonian assault on Jerusalem in 597 B.C.; he is living in exile in a town not far from Babylon. He thereafter sees through visions a series of dramatic events—including his being "transported" to Jerusalem, where he describes things in great detail. Thus the scene shifts through the book from Babylon to Jerusalem and back.

**Contents**   I. The calls and commission of Ezekiel (1–3)
  II. Conditions in Jerusalem just before the fall (4–24)
    A. The coming of the end
    B. The Temple defiled with idolatry
    C. Jerusalem forsaken by God
    D. False prophets condemned
    E. The call to repentance
  III. God's judgment on Judah's neighbors (25–32)
  IV. Words of comfort and hope after the fall of Jerusalem (33–39)
  V. Descriptions of the new Jerusalem (40–48)

# DANIEL

**Author**   Daniel presents a perplexing problem. Was the book written by Daniel, who was carried to Babylon in 605 B.C.? Did he at that time behold a vision of future oppression under Antiochus Epiphanes (c. 168 B.C.)? Or did some unknown writer in that later time actually write this story of a Daniel who had lived in Jerusalem during the Babylonian invasion? The evidence points to the latter; The Book of Daniel likely is the work of an unknown, later author.

**Date of Writing**   Around 168 B.C., during the Syrian oppression under Antiochus Epiphanes. In the Hebrew Bible, Daniel is not among the Prophets but among the Writings. (The canon of the Prophets had been fixed by 200 B.C.) The Hebrew itself is quite late, and parts of the book are written in Aramaic.

**Purpose**   The Book of Daniel is apocalyptic literature. An apocalypse is "an uncovering of the hidden," a revelation, a vision of the coming of God to redeem his people from their oppression. This book is an appeal for faithfulness in the midst of adversity: God has saved his people in times past, and he is now about to deliver them again.

**Setting**   The book begins with the first deportation of Jews to Babylon in 605 B.C. Daniel is among them, and subsequent events in his life in Babylon are described. There follows a description of Daniel's visions, in which he beholds the history of the Jews for the next four centuries.

**Contents**   I. The life of Daniel (1–6)
       A. The deportation and training of Daniel
       B. The interpretation of the king's dream
       C. The faith of Shadrach, Meshach, Abednego
       D. Other dreams and visions
       E. Daniel in the lions' den
    II. The visions of Daniel (7–12)

# HOSEA

**Author**  The book was written by Hosea, one of the twelve Minor Prophets (so-called only because their books were relatively short). The Book of Hosea probably includes later additions made by one of the prophet's disciples.

**Date of Writing**  The prophecies of Hosea span the years from 750 to 720 B.C. Hosea was a younger contemporary of the prophet Amos.

**Purpose**  To proclaim the faithfulness of God's love to a faithless people and to lead them to repentance.

**Setting**  Hosea prophesied in the last days of the Northern Kingdom, just before the fall of Samaria in 722 B.C. Hosea prophesied not only with words but with actions: at the command of God he married a harlot, in order to demonstrate God's relationship with an unfaithful nation. To the children born of this union he gave strikingly unusual names which announced that God's judgment was imminent.

**Contents**  I. Israel in its faithlessness is likened to an unfaithful wife (1–3)
>     A. Hosea's marriage to Gomer
>     B. Their children are named to bear witness to God

>    II. God's judgment promised in Israel (4–8)
>     A. Israel's abandonment of God
>     B. The call to repentance
>     C. Israel's refusal to respond
>     D. Disaster foretold

>    III. God's justice (9–14)
>     A. The exile predicted
>     B. The persistence of sin
>     C. God as Israel's only hope

# JOEL

**Author**  Joel, one of the twelve Minor Prophets.

**Date of Writing**  Uncertain. This short book is usually thought to come from the postexilic period, and perhaps was written between 500 and 350 B.C.

**Purpose**  To call the people to repentance before the coming Day of the Lord. The Day of the Lord is that day when God will at last appear and establish his justice among the nations. He will triumph over his foes, free his people from their oppressors, and establish social justice upon the earth. But he will also judge the people for their sins and punish the unrighteous, both Jew and Gentile. As such, the Day of the Lord becomes a day of dread and impending doom. Foretold by many of the prophets (Amos, Isaiah, and others), it is the day envisioned in the New Testament as "that day" or "the day of Jesus Christ," in which the Kingdom of Heaven will be established.

**Setting**  Unknown. The location of the valley of Jehoshaphat in 3:2 is unknown. From 3:1 it is likely that both Israel and Judah had fallen when this prophecy was spoken.

**Contents**  I. The plague of locusts: a judgment from God (1)
II. The coming Day of the Lord (2:1–11)
III. A call to repentance (2:12–17)
IV. The mercy of God (2:18–32)
V. God will judge the nations (3)

# AMOS

**Author**   Amos, one of the twelve Minor Prophets. Amos preached in Israel, the Northern Kingdom. His call came about 750 B.C.

**Date of Writing**   Uncertain; however, the book probably dates from the time of the original prophecies of Amos.

**Purpose**   To call a decadent Israel to repentance in the face of a coming judgment; to announce that in that day only a remnant would be spared.

**Setting**   Amos was a native of the Southern Kingdom, from the town of Tekoa, south of Jerusalem. He was a shepherd, with no formal religious training. He was one day called by God to go north, to Bethel in Israel, and to preach at that shrine against the full magnitude of Israel's sin. The whole prophecy may have been delivered over a two-day period in 750 B.C.

**Contents**   I. Introduction (1–2)
   A. The condemnation of Damascus, Philistia, Tyre, Edom, Ammon, Moab, Judah
   B. The condemnation of Israel itself
II. The people to be judged (3–6)
   A. God's punishment deserved
   B. Israel's failure to understand
   C. Exhortation to repentance
   D. The Day of the Lord
III. Visions of judgment (7:1–9:7)
   A. The locusts
   B. The fire
   C. The plumb line
   D. The summer fruit
   E. The fallen sanctuary
IV. A remnant to be spared (9:8–15)

# OBADIAH

**Author**  Obadiah, one of the twelve Minor Prophets.

**Date of Writing**  Uncertain; probably around 500 B.C.

**Purpose**  To condemn the Edomites, the southern neighbors of Israel, at a time when they were conspiring with Israel's foes. The Edomites were thought to be descendants of Esau; the old animosity between Esau and Jacob had continued through the centuries. Obadiah foretells the coming of judgment upon Edom.

**Setting**  Written after the exile, but before Edom was destroyed in the fifth century B.C., the book deals with Edom's delight at Judah's sufferings at the time of the fall of Jerusalem.

**Contents**  Only one chapter long, Obadiah may be outlined as follows:

    I.  The coming destruction of Edom (vs. 1–9)

    II.  The reason: failure to support Judah in its crisis (vs. 10–11)

    III.  A warning against gloating over the misfortunes of Judah (vs. 12–14)

    IV.  The Day of the Lord to deliver God's people (vs. 15–21)

# JONAH

**Author**  Unknown. A prophet by the name of Jonah is referred to in II Kings 14:25, but the events in this book occurred much later. This book, and the Jonah of whom it tells, is included among the twelve Minor Prophets.

**Date of Writing**  Because of its implication that Nineveh had already fallen (3:3 says that "Nineveh *was* an exceedingly great city"), the story would be set no earlier than 612 B.C., when the city was destroyed. The Hebrew of the text also indicates a late date of writing, perhaps some time after the exile, between 500 and 350 B.C.

**Purpose**  The book demonstrates how difficult it is for us to accept God's forgiveness of the sins of others. The book also reminds the reader that God loves and will forgive repentant sinners in every nation.

**Setting**  The story begins in Palestine, where God calls Jonah to go and preach at Nineveh, the capital of Assyria, to the far northeast of Palestine. Instead, Jonah boards a ship and starts across the Mediterranean; he then returns to Palestine, goes to Nineveh, and preaches there. The story ends with Jonah in dejection over Nineveh's repentance.

**Contents**  I. God's call and Jonah's disobedience (1)
  - A. A call to preach at Nineveh
  - B. Jonah flees, bound for Tarshish (Spain)
  - C. The tempest and the great fish

  II. Jonah's thanksgiving for deliverance (2)

  III. Jonah's message and its results (3–4)
  - A. The repentance of Nineveh
  - B. The city is forgiven and spared by God
  - C. Jonah's anguish

# MICAH

**Author**   Micah, one of the twelve Minor Prophets. Micah lived in the Southern Kingdom and was a younger contemporary of Isaiah.

**Date of Writing**   The first verse dates Micah's ministry between 740 and 687 B.C. While the present book may contain more than just the words of Micah, the whole book seems to date from that period.

**Purpose**   Prophesying in the Southern Kingdom at the time when the Northern Kingdom was falling, Micah says that God's judgment will come to Judah as well, but that God will show mercy if the people repent.

**Setting**   Micah prophesied in the country at Moresheth, near Gath, at the same time that Isaiah was preaching in the city of Jerusalem. His earliest words foretell the fall of Samaria and must therefore have been spoken before 722 B.C.

**Contents**   I. The judgment of God on both Israel and Judah (1–3)
          II. God to restore his people (4–5)
          III. God's controversy with his people (6–7)

# NAHUM

**Author**  Nahum, one of the twelve Minor Prophets.

**Date of Writing**  Probably around 615 B.C., between the siege of Nineveh by the Medes in 623 B.C. and its final destruction by the Babylonians in 612 B.C.

**Purpose**  Delivered to the people of Judah, this is a prophecy of the impending doom of Nineveh, the capital of Assyria. It is a message to console the Jews who lived in constant dread of the Assyrians, who had destroyed the Northern Kingdom a century earlier.

**Setting**  The book gives no details of its background, except that it is a vision of "Nahum of Elkosh." The latter was probably a village in Palestine.

**Contents**  This short book may be outlined as follows:

    I. The majesty of God (1)
        A. God's mighty acts
        B. His people to be freed
    II. Judgment upon Nineveh (2–3)
        A. The fall of the city
        B. Words of woe to Nineveh

# HABAKKUK

**Author**  Habakkuk, one of the twelve Minor Prophets.

**Date of Writing**  The prophecy was probably delivered after the fall of Nineveh to the Chaldeans in 612 B.C., and before the Chaldeans (Babylonians) had fully established themselves as the leading world power (1:6).

**Purpose**  To offer an answer to the question: How could God allow such punishment of his people as they had endured under Assyria and might yet face from Babylonia? Habakkuk says, "The righteous shall live by his faith."

**Setting**  The prophecy of Habakkuk was obviously delivered to the people of Judah at the time mentioned above, but we have no other details about the background of this book. The book is in the form of a vision and a prayer.

**Contents**  I. The complaint of Habakkuk (1)
    A. The success of the wicked
    B. The Chaldeans as instruments of God
    C. A cry against violence
  II. The answer of God (2)
    A. The watchtower of the prophet
    B. The salvation of the faithful
    C. God's ultimate victory
  III. The prophet's prayer (3)

# ZEPHANIAH

**Author**   Zephaniah, one of the twelve Minor Prophets. Zephaniah was a prophet in Judah, the Southern Kingdom.

**Date of Writing**   During the reign of Josiah (1:1), probably before that king's program of reformation in 621 B.C.

**Purpose**   To call the people from their false optimism that prosperity was near, and to announce the coming terrible Day of the Lord.

**Setting**   Zephaniah was an inhabitant of Jerusalem who, incensed at the decay and depravity about him, called the people to repentance.

**Contents**   I. The Day of the Lord (1)
    A. The terror of that day
    B. Judah to be judged
    C. The nearness of judgment
  II. God to judge the nations (2)
  III. The condemnation of Jerusalem (3:1–7)
  IV. A remnant to be spared (3:8–20)

# HAGGAI

**Author**  Haggai, one of the twelve Minor Prophets.

**Date of Writing**  The Book of Haggai was written in 520 B.C., at the same time as the book (and prophecies) of Zechariah.

**Purpose**  To summon the people to put first things first and rebuild the Temple of the Lord.

**Setting**  Following the destruction of Jerusalem in 586 B.C., the people had been carried into exile. When they returned home almost fifty years later, they found the city still lying in ruins. Slowly they began rebuilding, but for twenty years they ignored the fallen House of God. In 520 B.C. both Haggai and Zechariah set about to exhort the people to rebuild.

**Contents**  This book has only two chapters, comprised of four separate sections, each dated with the occasion of its delivery.

    I. The call to rebuild the Temple, and the people's response (1)

    II. The greater glory of the new Temple described (2:1–9)

    III. The assurance of God's coming blessing (2:10–19)

    IV. God's blessing upon Zerubbabel (2:20–23)

# ZECHARIAH

**Author**  Zechariah, one of the twelve Minor Prophets, and a contemporary of Haggai.

**Date of Writing**  Zechariah began preaching in 520 B.C., several months after the message of Haggai had been completed. He delivered a series of visions and prophecies in 519–518 B.C. The latter part of the book (9–14) is generally believed to come from a later period.

**Purpose**  To inspire men to trust in God's promises and to rebuild their lives in response to that trust.

**Setting**  Following Haggai's call to rebuild the fallen Temple in 520 B.C., Zechariah was called to preach to the people in Jerusalem. This he did through a series of visions. A number of oracles concerning the future follow those visions.

**Contents**  I. Introduction and visions (1:1–6:8)
- A. The lesson of the past
- B. The vision of the horsemen
- C. The four horns and the four smiths
- D. The measuring line
- E. The high priest and Satan
- F. The lampstand and the olive trees
- G. The flying scroll
- H. The woman
- I. The four chariots

II. Crowning of the high priest (6:9–15)
III. Additional prophecies (7–8)
IV. Oracles about the Kingdom of God (9–11)
V. Oracles about Jerusalem (12–14)

# MALACHI

**Author**  Malachi, the last of the twelve Minor Prophets. His name means "my messenger." Some have suggested that this was not the name but rather the title of the prophet.

**Date of Writing**  No evidence is given in the book as to who Malachi is, or exactly when the book was written. However, from the content we discover that the second Temple had been built, and the religious zeal of the era of reconstruction had passed. We can therefore date the book around 450–430 B.C.

**Purpose**  Seeing the people's hollow religious life, Malachi calls upon the people to stop cheating God, and to restore righteousness to their religious life. He announces the coming judgment on the terrible Day of the Lord (see on Joel).

**Setting**  The prophecy of Malachi was delivered in Jerusalem sometime in the fifth century B.C., possibly during the absence of Nehemiah in 433 B.C.

**Contents**  I. Israel's disregard for the love of God (1–2)
- A. Israel's ingratitude
- B. Blemished offerings condemned
- C. Faithlessness denounced

II. The coming of God's messenger (3–4)
- A. God's messenger to purify
- B. A call for full tithes
- C. The faithful remnant spared
- D. The Day of the Lord foretold

# Between the Testaments

THE PERIOD between the end of the Old Testament and the beginning of the New Testament is often overlooked by students of the Bible.

Because we usually have but a passing interest in what happened to the Jews in the centuries just before Christ, the period between the Testaments is easily ignored. Yet this was a period when great changes shook the whole world, including Palestine, and those changes are worth our attention.

## THE WORLD OF THE TIMES

To understand this intertestamental period, a brief review of world events is in order. Nebuchadnezzar and the Babylonians had conquered Jerusalem in 586 B.C. and had taken many of the Jews into captivity. But in 539 B.C., Babylonia was in turn defeated by the Persians, who permitted the Jews to return home. The Persian Empire at this point stretched from India to Greece, where its western push was stopped with the defeat of King Darius I by the Athenians at Marathon (490 B.C.). Ten years later, Sparta defeated another Persian army under Xerxes I, Darius' son, and gradually but irreversibly the influence of the Greek city-states spread outward until it peaked with the conquests of Alexander the Great (son of Philip of Macedon), who crushed the Persians in 331 B.C.

After the death of Alexander, his empire crumbled. In time, three large pieces emerged: Macedonia (north of Greece), Syria, and Egypt. Palestine was placed under Egyptian jurisdiction, but in 198 B.C. Antiochus the Great of Syria defeated Egypt and gained control of Palestine. Syria in turn fell to Rome in 64 B.C.

## PALESTINE BETWEEN THE TESTAMENTS

When Cyrus permitted the Jews to return to Palestine (538 B.C.), they found the land totally ravaged by war. Slowly they began to rebuild. During the reign of Darius, a new Temple was erected, houses were built, and farms were cultivated again. Artaxerxes I, son of Xerxes I (the latter was the Ahasuerus of The Book of Esther), permitted Ezra to lead more refugees back to Jerusalem and allowed Nehemiah to rebuild the city walls.

During this period there was relative freedom of religion. But with Antiochus and the Syrians came a terrible repression, including the plunder of the Temple itself in 168 B.C.

## THE MACCABEAN REVOLT

Some of the most important events of the whole intertestamental period revolved about the family of Judas Maccabeus. The father, Mattathias, an aged priest, was so incensed by the defilement of the Temple by the Syrians that he sparked an armed revolt. With his sons and other dedicated followers he fled to the mountains, where the group began guerrilla warfare. The leader of the guerrillas was Judas (Maccabeus is a nickname meaning "hammerhead," perhaps describing his persistence). Under Judas the people drove the Syrians out of Jerusalem, purified the Temple, and reinstituted the daily sacrifice. A winter feast to commemorate this victory was initiated and has been kept annually ever since (Hanukkah). Judas fell in battle in 160 B.C. and was succeeded in turn by his brothers.

An era of relative independence was achieved, but subsequent internal struggles among descendants of the Maccabees finally erupted into civil war, around 65 B.C. An appeal was made to Rome for help, and help came, at a price: the nation of Judah became the Roman province of Judea. The Jewish kings became figureheads, and the real power of government was lodged in the Roman procurator.

## THE APOCRYPHA

During this period between the Testaments, another body of religious writings appeared. Known as the Apocrypha ("hidden things"), these sixteen books were later judged noncanonical by the rabbis, but they are important for the information they give about the period. The books are: I and II Esdras (Greek for Ezra; containing other stories about the fall of Jerusalem); Tobit; Judith (the story of a faithful widow); The Additions to the Book of Esther; The Wisdom of Solomon; Ecclesiasticus (a book concerning wisdom); Baruch; The Prayer of Azariah and the Song of the Three Young Men; Susanna; Bel and the Dragon; The Prayer of Manasseh; and I, II, III, and IV Maccabees (which deal with the Maccabean revolt).

# The New Testament:
# An Introduction

## THE STORY OF THE NEW TESTAMENT

TAKEN AS A WHOLE, the New Testament is at once a biography, a history, and a discourse on theology. It is, of course, the story of the life and ministry of Jesus of Nazareth. It is also the story of how that ministry was continued through the creation of the church. And it is the record of how that church conceived its mission and responded to Christ's presence within its ongoing life.

The entire New Testament covers a period of approximately 130 years, beginning with the annunciation of the birth of John the Baptist in 6 B.C., and concluding with the writing of II Peter, as late as A.D. 125.

The Old Testament seems to end in failure, with only the hope that salvation would come at some future time through the faithful remnant that God had spared.

The New Testament is the sudden, dramatic announcement by God that the promise is fulfilled; that with the appearance of his Son, a New Covenant, a New Testament, is proposed. It is a covenant of life, an invitation to live life in fullness now, and to escape death forever, through Jesus Christ! This is the Gospel, the good news that death is destroyed.

## THE FOUR GOSPEL ACCOUNTS

There is only one gospel message, but it is presented in four different books called Gospels: Matthew, Mark, Luke, and John. The first three of these present a common viewpoint and are sometimes called the Synoptics, a word based on a Greek term meaning "looked at together." In general, Matthew, Mark, and Luke concentrate on Jesus' public ministry as he traveled through Galilee, and on his suffering, death, and resurrection. On the other hand, The Gospel of John, sometimes called "the spiritual Gospel," also presents experiences and interpretations and discussions of Jesus with his disciples during his ministry in Judea. Thus the record of what

61

Jesus taught and said and did can only be appreciated through the combined accounts of four separate books.

In the Old Testament, God had revealed himself through the prophets and the life of the nation Israel. In the New Testament, God makes a final revelation of himself through his Son. In the life of Christ, we see and know God as he is.

The facts of that life are familiar and brief: born in a stable, Jesus lived in obscurity until he began his ministry. After three years of preaching, teaching, and healing, he was arrested, condemned, and nailed to a cross. He died and was buried, but on the third day he rose from the dead. And in that resurrection we finally perceive the full scope of God's promise: "For God so loved the world that he gave his only Son, that whoever believes in him should not perish but have eternal life."

## THE ACTS OF THE APOSTLES

The resurrection is not the end of the New Testament story, for once the risen Lord had ascended into heaven, God did not leave his people helpless. On the Day of Pentecost, he sent the Holy Spirit to create and empower the church (ecclesia: literally, "that which is called out"). The Acts of the Apostles is the story of that church. It tells of the dramatic conversion of Paul, and how he became the preeminent missionary of his time. It tells of the hardship and persecution suffered by the early Christians. It describes how the gospel was taken to the Gentiles; how the church in time began to lose its Jewish character; and how, long before the end of the first century, the church had spread the gospel of Jesus Christ across the Mediterranean world from Jerusalem to Rome.

## THE NEW TESTAMENT LETTERS AND REVELATION

The rest of the New Testament is composed of twenty-one letters (epistles) and The Revelation to John. The letters are concerned with various questions of faith and practice with which the early church was confronted. They fall into three categories: Paul's letters to various churches (also including Hebrews, Philemon); Paul's letters to his assistants, known as the pastoral epistles (I, II Timothy; Titus); and the so-called catholic, or general, epistles, most of them written to the church at large (James; I, II Peter; I, II, III John; Jude).

Revelation, also called The Apocalypse ("an uncovering"), is a series of visions of the future. (Apocalyptic literature is found elsewhere in the Bible, for example, Matthew 24–25, and The Book of Daniel.) The soaring imagery of Revelation, reaffirming the fulfillment of God's promises, makes a fitting climax to the Bible.

# New Testament Chronology

## EVENTS IN THE LIFE OF CHRIST

| | |
|---|---|
| 6 B.C. | Foretelling of John the Baptist's birth |
| 5 B.C. | Annunciation to Mary of Jesus' birth |
| | Birth of John the Baptist |
| | Birth of Jesus (Late 5 B.C. or early 4 B.C.)* |
| 4 B.C. | Jesus presented in the Temple |
| | Visit of Wise Men; flight into Egypt |
| | Return from Egypt to Nazareth |
| A.D. 8 | Jesus' visit to the Temple at age twelve |
| A.D. 27 | Baptism of Jesus; temptation in wilderness |
| | First miracle (Cana) |
| | First Passover (Jerusalem) |
| | Jesus preaches in Judea |
| | Jesus returns to Galilee via Samaria |
| A.D. 28 | Beginning of Jesus' public ministry (Galilee) |
| | First disciples called |
| | Return of Jesus to Jerusalem for second Passover |
| | The Sermon on the Mount (Galilee) |
| | Healing, preaching ministry of Jesus (Galilee) |
| | Teaching of parables: sower, tares, pearl |
| | Sending of the Twelve |
| | John the Baptist beheaded |
| A.D. 29 | Third Passover observed (Galilee) |
| | Syrophoenician girl and others healed |
| | Foretelling by Jesus of his death |
| | Sending of the Seventy; departure for Judea |
| | Visit of Jesus to Mary and Martha (Bethany) |
| A.D. 30 | Ministry of Jesus beyond Jordan |
| | Lazarus raised from the dead |
| | Palm Sunday: triumphal entry into Jerusalem |
| |    Monday: Cleansing of the Temple |
| |    Thursday: The Last Supper (last Passover) |

Friday: Jesus' trial and crucifixion
Easter Sunday: Resurrection of Jesus
Resurrection appearances
Ascension of Jesus (forty days after Easter)
*NOTE:   In the sixth century A.D., Dionysius Exiguus set the date of Jesus' birth at A.D. 1, but most scholars now think that to be in error, and place the date between 6 and 4 B.C.

### FURTHER NEW TESTAMENT EVENTS

| | |
|---|---|
| 30 | Day of Pentecost; church empowered by the Holy Spirit |
| 35? | Conversion of Saul of Tarsus (Paul) |
| 37 | First visit of Paul to Jerusalem as a Christian |
| 37–45 | Paul's early ministry (Tarsus area) |
| 44–46 | Paul at Antioch, then Jerusalem |
| 45? (60?) | James written |
| 46–48 | Paul's first missionary journey |
| c. 50 | Church council (Jerusalem) |
| 51–53 | Paul's second missionary journey |
| c. 52 | I, II Thessalonians, Galatians written |
| 54–58 | Paul's third missionary journey |
| 56 | I Corinthians written |
| 57 | II Corinthians written |
| 58 | Romans written |
| | Paul arrested |
| 58–60 | Paul's imprisonment (Caesarea) |
| 60 | Appeal to Festus; Paul in Rome |
| 61 | Paul at Rome, imprisoned |
| 62 | Ephesians, Colossians, Philemon written |
| 63 | Philippians written |
| 63–64 | Paul's release from prison |
| 64 | I Timothy written |
| 65 | Mark, Titus, I Peter? written |
| 67 | Rearrest of Paul |
| 67 | II Timothy written |
| 68? | Deaths of Peter and Paul (Rome) |
| c. 75 | Matthew, Luke written |
| c. 77 | Acts written |
| c. 85 | Hebrews written |
| c. 90–100 (or earlier) | Gospel of John written |

90 and later:  Jude, Revelation, I, II, III John, and II Peter written

NOTE:   All dates in the life of Paul are approximate, and are fixed in relation to the accession of Festus as procurator of Judea, either A.D. 58 or A.D. 60. This chronology is based upon the later date.

# The Books
## of the New Testament

### MATTHEW

**Author**  Matthew, one of the twelve apostles (also called Levi), probably wrote this Gospel, although the book itself does not name its author. Before becoming an apostle, Matthew had been a tax collector.

**Date of Writing**  Approximately A.D. 75. Matthew borrows freely from Mark. Ninety percent of Mark is included in Matthew; Matthew also follows Mark's chronology of events. (In addition to using Mark, Matthew also probably drew from a collection of "Sayings of Jesus" that no longer exists.) The dating of Matthew depends, therefore, on when Mark was written; there are arguments for suggesting a later date for Matthew, but A.D. 75 seems the most likely.

**Purpose**  To set forth the life of Christ in such a way as to show how he fulfills the Old Testament expectation of a Messiah.

**Setting**  The book begins with an introductory genealogy, tracing the ancestors of Jesus from Abraham through David. Matthew begins the story of Jesus' life with his birth in 5 B.C. and ends just after the resurrection in A.D. 30.

**Contents**  I.  Birth and infancy of Jesus (1–2)
     II.  Jesus' baptism and temptation (3–4)
    III.  The Sermon on the Mount (5–7)
    IV.  Jesus' ministry of healing and teaching (8–18)
     V.  The last days of his ministry (19–25)
        A.  Teaching on marriage; prediction of the cross
        B.  Palm Sunday and cleansing of the Temple
        C.  Signs of the end of the world
    VI.  Crucifixion, death, and resurrection (26–28)

# MARK

**Author**  John Mark, a kinsman of Barnabas, who accompanied Paul and Barnabas on Paul's first missionary journey. Mark was a Jew from Jerusalem who later became an associate of Peter.

**Date of Writing**  About A.D. 65. Irenaeus (one of the early church fathers) says that Mark wrote his record of the gospel after the deaths of Peter and Paul (A.D. 68?).

**Purpose**  Mark was addressed to those who were already Christians, to give them a brief narrative of the facts concerning Jesus of Nazareth. It was written for Greek-speaking Christians who were scattered throughout the Mediterranean world.

**Setting**  Mark was probably not one of the original followers of Jesus. But he would have gained much firsthand information from his association with Peter. We are not certain of the sources of his information, but at some point, Mark compiled his own written account of the gospel of Jesus Christ. He omits the details of Jesus' birth and begins with Jesus' baptism in A.D. 27.

**Contents**  I. The Galilean ministry (1:1–8:26)
    A. Baptism of Jesus
    B. Beginning of Jesus' ministry in Galilee
    C. Opposition develops
    D. Parables of Jesus
    E. Sending of the Twelve
    F. Jesus' visit to Tyre and Sidon
  II. The Judean ministry (8:27–13:37)
    A. The announcement of his coming death
    B. The journey from Galilee to Judea
    C. Palm Sunday; cleansing of the Temple
    D. Further teachings in Judea
  III. The last week: death and resurrection (14–16)

# LUKE

**Author**  Luke, a physician, who accompanied Paul on his second missionary journey. Luke was a Gentile.

**Date of Writing**  Probably around A.D. 75. Luke's second volume, The Acts of the Apostles, was completed shortly thereafter. Luke borrows from Mark (one third of the book comes from Mark), from the now-lost "Sayings of Jesus," and other sources.

**Purpose**  Luke states his purpose (1:3–4): "To write an orderly account (of the things which have been accomplished among us) . . . that you may know the truth of the things of which you have been informed."

**Setting**  Luke begins with the annunciation (6 B.C.) of the birth of John the Baptist; he details the birth and life of Jesus; and he ends just prior to Jesus' ascension, probably in May, A.D. 30.

**Contents**  I. Jesus' early years (1–2)
   II. The preparation for ministry (3:1–4:13)
      A. Baptism of Jesus
      B. Temptation in the wilderness
   III. The ministry in Galilee (4:14–9:50)
      A. Jesus rejected at Nazareth
      B. The Twelve called
      C. A ministry of teaching and healing
   IV. The way to Jerusalem (9:51–19:27)
      A. The sending of the Seventy
      B. Parables and teachings
      C. Religious leaders denounced
   V. Jerusalem: the last days (19:28–24:53)
      A. The Temple: cleansing and teaching
      B. The Last Supper
      C. The Crucifixion
      D. Resurrection and post-Easter appearances

# JOHN

**Author**   Probably John, one of the twelve apostles, the "beloved disciple," son of Zebedee and brother of James. But see I John, "Author."

**Date of Writing**   John's Gospel is traditionally dated between A.D. 90 and A.D. 100, or even later. Yet some argue for a date as early as A.D. 65. From the text it seems likely that the book was written before the second Temple was destroyed by the Romans in A.D. 70. And if John was martyred in A.D. 70 (as tradition holds), this book would have been written earlier.

**Purpose**   John tells us, in 20:31: "these [signs] are written that you may believe that Jesus is the Christ, the Son of God, and that believing you may have life in his name."

**Setting**   John's Gospel is primarily concerned with the Judean (southern) ministry of Jesus, while Matthew, Mark, and Luke focus largely on his ministry around Galilee. In the Galilean ministry, Jesus was usually surrounded by crowds; John tells us more of Jesus' private life and ministry with his disciples. He begins (after the prologue) with Jesus' baptism, and he ends with Jesus' meetings with the disciples following the resurrection.

**Contents**   I. The prologue (1:1–18)
II. Jesus' baptism and early ministry in Galilee (1:19–2:12)
III. The first Passover in Jerusalem, ministry in Judea, and return to Galilee (2:13–4:54)
IV. Twice again from Galilee to Jerusalem (5:1–7:9)
V. From Galilee to Judea and Transjordan (7:10–10:42)
VI. Return to Judea (11)
VII. The last week (12–21)

# THE ACTS

**Author**   Luke, author of The Gospel of Luke. He was a physician and a Gentile.

**Date of Writing**   Probably in A.D. 77, several years after Luke wrote his Gospel, the "first book" of Acts 1:1. Theophilus, to whom both books are addressed, means "lover of God"; it is not known if this was an actual person or simply the way Luke addresses anyone who seeks God in these pages.

**Purpose**   In ch. 1:1–4 of his Gospel, Luke states that he is attempting to present an orderly account of the events of Christ's life. In this later volume, he continues the story after the ascension of Jesus, relating how the early church was born and grew until at last it had spread across the Mediterranean world.

**Setting**   The Acts of the Apostles begins in A.D. 30 with the ascension of Jesus into heaven. The early chapters trace the founding and early days of the church in Jerusalem; later the account shifts to follow the missionary career of the apostle Paul.

**Contents**   I. The church in Jerusalem (1:1–6:7)
  II. The church in Palestine (6:8–9:31)
      A. Stephen's martyrdom
      B. The persecution under Saul
      C. Saul's conversion on the road to Damascus
  III. The church at Antioch (9:32–12:24)
      A. The gospel preached to Gentiles
  IV. The gospel in Asia Minor and Europe (12:25–21:16)
      A. Paul's first missionary journey (12:25–14:28)
      B. The Council of Jerusalem (c. A.D. 50) (15:1–35)
      C. Paul's second missionary journey (15:36–18:22)
      D. Paul's third missionary journey (18:23–21:16)
  V. Journey to Rome (21:17–28:31)

# ROMANS

**Author** The apostle Paul.

**Date of Writing** A.D. 58, probably from Corinth, while Paul was completing his third missionary journey.

**Purpose** To set forth to the church at Rome Paul's understanding of the gospel of Jesus Christ.

**Setting** The church at Rome apparently was already quite sizable when this letter was written. We do not know who founded the Roman church; certainly it was not Paul, nor is it likely to have been Peter. But Rome was the seat of the empire, and the church in Rome held the key to the spread of Christianity. Thus, it seems, Paul was moved to set forth in this, his longest letter, a complete and logical statement of the gospel: what it is, and how it saves lives.

**Contents**
  I. Paul's credentials (1:1–17)
  II. The need: our inability to save ourselves (1:18–3:20)
    A. Both Jew and Gentile guilty
    B. All convicted by the law
  III. The answer: God's gift of salvation (3:21–5:21)
    A. Justification by faith
    B. Adam and Christ contrasted
  IV. Life in Christ described (6–8)
    A. Freedom in Christ
    B. The transforming power of the Spirit
  V. Israel chosen for salvation (9–11)
    A. Israel's rejection of God
    B. Israel still to be saved
  VI. The results of the gospel (12–16)
    A. Obedience to authorities discussed
    B. Love and law contrasted
    C. Christians not to be stumbling blocks

# I CORINTHIANS

**Author**  The apostle Paul.

**Date of Writing**  A.D. 56 or 57; written to the church at Corinth (Greece), which Paul had founded on his second missionary journey. I Corinthians was written from Ephesus, near the end of Paul's third missionary journey.

**Purpose**  In an earlier letter (see 5:9) Paul had written the Corinthians concerning immorality within the church. A reply (see 7:1) had come to Paul from Corinth, raising new questions. In response, Paul wrote this letter to speak to certain problems within the church, and to answer specific questions that the Corinthians had raised.

**Setting**  This letter reflects the struggles of the new church in Corinth, which was a bustling city set at a crossroads of commerce. Corinth at the time was infected with every kind of immoral practice. The need for Christians to stand apart from immorality is a primary concern of this letter. Not only was Paul apparently dissatisfied with the Corinthians' reply to his earlier letter, but "Chloe's people" (1:11) had brought him personal news of division and immorality within the church. Thus this letter came to be written.

**Contents**  I. Greetings and thanksgiving (1:1–9)
    II. Paul's judgments on disorders (1:10–6:20)
        A. Division within the church
        B. The apostolic ministry
        C. Need for purity and honor
    III. Paul's answers to questions raised (7–15)
        A. Marriage and divorce
        B. Food offered to idols
        C. Gifts of the Spirit
        D. The resurrection of the body
    IV. News and closing (16)

# II CORINTHIANS

**Author**  The apostle Paul.

**Date of Writing**  Late in A.D. 57; written from Macedonia after a brief but painful visit that Paul had paid the Corinthian church after writing I Corinthians.

**Purpose**  I. To heal the wounds of a divided church
II. To call it to contribute for the church at Jerusalem
III. To defend Paul's own apostleship

**Setting**  After writing I Corinthians (see the preceding page for details which occasioned that letter), Paul learned that conditions in Corinth had worsened, and that the church was badly split. Sometime in A.D. 57 he made a quick visit to Corinth (implied by 13:1 ff.), where he was humiliated. He returned to Ephesus and wrote a "severe" letter (inferred from 2:3–9 and 7:8). That letter was possibly delivered by Titus. (II Cor. 10–13 is thought to be a part of that now-missing letter.) The news from Corinth improved thereafter; on his way to Corinth one final time, Paul met Titus in Macedonia. Titus reported that the situation was healing. From Macedonia Paul wrote this letter (II Corinthians). He subsequently arrived at Corinth (Acts 20:2), and from there he wrote his Letter to the Romans.

**Contents**  I. Paul's relation to the church (1–7)
A. A call to forgive the repentant sinner
B. The ministry of reconciliation described
C. Joy at repentance
II. The collection for Jerusalem (8–9)
III. Paul's defense of his apostleship (10–13)
A. Signs of a true ministry
B. The sustaining power of Christ

# GALATIANS

**Author**  The apostle Paul.

**Date of Writing**  About A.D. 52, during Paul's second missionary journey. Paul probably wrote from Corinth.

**Purpose**  To set the Galatian Christians free from the observance of nonessential, Jewish aspects of the Law.

**Setting**  As more and more Gentiles were added to the church, the question was raised increasingly as to whether or not they were bound by the Jewish Law: dietary laws, prescribed festivals, even circumcision itself. About A.D. 50, a council of church leaders had met in Jerusalem; their decision was that Gentiles were indeed able to become Christians without first becoming Jews. Yet in the churches at Lystra, Derbe, Antioch, and Iconium (in the Roman province of Galatia), which Paul had founded during his first missionary journey, the controversy had not been resolved. The church there had the Old Testament Scriptures, which required strict observance of the Law; against this they had only the word of Paul. Thus, hearing of their disagreement, Paul wrote to the churches in Galatia while he was at Corinth.

**Contents**  I. Paul's defense of his authority (1–2)
  A. The unity of the gospel
  B. Paul an apostle of that gospel
  C. The same gospel for the whole church
  II. Justification by faith (3:1–5:12)
  A. Faith and law contrasted
  B. Legalism deplored
  III. The life of faith described (5:13–6:18)

# EPHESIANS

**Author**   The apostle Paul.

**Date of Writing**   About A.D. 62. Ephesians was probably written from Rome during Paul's imprisonment there.

**Purpose**   This book is a magnificent summary of Paul's previous teachings about the nature and purpose of the church. It was—and is—worth the attention of every Christian. So succinct is its message that Paul may have made several copies of this letter, to be read within the churches of Asia Minor. The letter contains no reference to anything in Ephesus. Nor do the earliest and best manuscripts contain the words "at Ephesus" within the salutation, although later copies do. The explanation might be that Paul, wishing to instruct the church in what he perceived to be God's eternal purpose for his people, put down his thoughts in a general letter which was to be widely circulated. We happen to have preserved copies that bear the name "Ephesus."

**Setting**   Ephesians is a relatively brief letter with no formal structure. The thoughts of the author flow and sometimes soar as he is caught up in one majestic theme after another. It is a timeless exposition of God's plan of salvation, a letter addressed to the church in every age.

**Contents**   I. The church, the people elected by God (1–3)
   A. Mankind destined to live in Christ
   B. Mankind made one in Christ
   C. Jew and Gentile now one in Christ
II. A description of the Christian life (4–6)
   A. Various gifts in the body of Christ
   B. Correct Christian living described
   C. The armor of God for the Christian

# PHILIPPIANS

**Author**  The apostle Paul.

**Date of Writing**  A.D. 62 or 63, while Paul was imprisoned in Rome.

**Purpose**  To summon the church at Philippi to resolve their problems by living lives yielded to Christ.

**Setting**  Paul had founded the church at Philippi, and he had always held a particular fondness for these Christians. They had repeatedly sent gifts to support him while he worked in other cities; they had recently sent Epaphroditus with yet another gift for Paul during his Roman imprisonment. Epaphroditus had been instructed to remain with Paul, to assist him in whatever way he could. But Epaphroditus himself had fallen ill, and having now recovered, he was sent back to Philippi by Paul, bearing this letter for the church.

**Contents**

# COLOSSIANS

**Author**  The apostle Paul.

**Date of Writing**  A.D. 62, while Paul was imprisoned at Rome.

**Purpose**  To dissuade the Christians at Colossae from being led astray by teachers who insisted that "basic" Christianity was not enough.

**Setting**  News has come to Paul of the work of false teachers among the Christians at Colossae. These teachers have apparently been urging the Colossians to worship angels, to practice asceticism, and to observe special, secret rites as part of their Christian faith. Paul dispatches this letter to deal with the problem. In it he assures his readers that Christ alone is sufficient for every human need; that nothing more is needed, and nothing less.

**Contents**  I. The address (1:1–2)
II. Christ the center of the universe (1:3–14)
III. An exhortation to hold fast to the gospel (1:15–2:5)
IV. Warnings about false prophets (2:6–23)
V. The new life in Christ described (3:1–17; 4:2–6)
VI. Duties of the Christian family (3:18–4:1)
VII. Personal words (4:7–18)

# I THESSALONIANS

**Author**   The apostle Paul.

**Date of Writing**   About A.D. 52, probably from Corinth, during Paul's second missionary journey.

**Purpose**   I. To give thanks for the growth of the church at Thessalonica

    II. To address three specific concerns:

        A. Misconception of the doctrine of the Second Coming of Christ

        B. Misunderstanding concerning those Christians who had recently died

        C. Friction concerning church leaders with spiritual gifts

    III. To exhort the church

**Setting**   Earlier during the present missionary journey, Paul has founded the church at Thessalonica. His stay was very brief, and he has not as yet been able to return for a visit. He was forced to leave Thessalonica because of the hostility of the Jews; from Athens he sent Timothy back with words of encouragement. Now Timothy has returned with the good news that the Thessalonian church has continued to grow, even in the midst of hardship. But he also has reported several areas in the life of the church that Paul finds distressing. In response, Paul writes this letter.

**Contents**   I. Thankfulness for the Thessalonians (1)

    II. Reminder of Paul's ministry among them (2)

    III. Paul's absence and Timothy's visit (3)

    IV. Teachings on specific questions (4:1–5:24)

        A. Sexual purity

        B. Those who have recently died

        C. The Day of the Lord

        D. Respect for church leaders

    V. Closing (5:25–28)

# II THESSALONIANS

**Author**  The apostle Paul.

**Date of Writing**  A.D. 52 or 53, shortly after I Thessalonians had been written; from Corinth, during Paul's second missionary journey.

**Purpose**  To correct misconceptions held by the church at Thessalonica concerning the Second Coming of Christ, and to encourage the church to abandon idleness in its daily life.

**Setting**  The situation addressed in I Thessalonians did not immediately improve; indeed, it may have grown worse. Paul wrote this second letter only a few months after he had written the first. Again dealing with the problem of Christ's Second Coming, he tells them that Christ may not come soon. This time Paul depicts that coming day as one of judgment and condemnation, as well as salvation. The whole tone of this letter seems more stern than the first one. From 2:2, it appears that another letter may have been circulated, purportedly from Paul, containing false teaching about the Day of the Lord. Paul reminds his readers that "the rebellion" and other signs must come first.

**Contents**  I. Assurance of God's judgment (1)
　　　　　　II. The Day of the Lord (2:1–12)
　　　　　　III. An appeal for steadfastness (2:13–3:5)
　　　　　　IV. The necessity of daily discipline (3:6–15)

# I TIMOTHY

**Author**   The apostle Paul. There is, however, some question as to the authorship.

**Date of Writing**   Around A.D. 64. The date of writing would be late in Paul's life, probably during the years of freedom between Paul's Roman imprisonments. However, the authorship of this book (as well as II Timothy and Titus) has long been disputed because of differences in vocabulary from all Paul's earlier letters.

**Purpose**   The first of the "pastoral" epistles, I Timothy was written to prepare the church and its officers to minister in the name of Jesus Christ.

**Setting**   Timothy had been left in charge of the church at Ephesus while Paul went to Macedonia (1:3). If Paul was in fact released from prison in Rome in A.D. 63 or 64 and journeyed through Macedonia, this would likely be the time when this letter was written. It was written to provide Timothy with a guide for handling the difficulties he faced in the Ephesian church.

**Contents**   I. Instructions for the church (1–3)
  A. Warnings about false teachers
  B. Instructions concerning worship
  C. Instructions about church officers
  II. Advice to Timothy (4–6)
  A. The problem of false doctrine
  B. Dealing with various groups in the church
  C. Concluding words

# II TIMOTHY

**Author**  The apostle Paul. There is, however, some question as to the authorship.

**Date of Writing**  Around A.D. 66 or 67. This letter was written from Rome during Paul's final imprisonment, not long before his death.

**Purpose**  The second of the "pastoral" epistles, this letter was written to advise Timothy in his work as an evangelist and teacher, and to ask him to come to Rome.

**Setting**  Paul's imprisonment stems from his being charged as an evil-doer; he has already endured one trial (4:16–17), and now he feels that he is about to face martyrdom. He says, "I have fought the good fight, I have finished the race, I have kept the faith." Yet even in the despair of his situation, Paul remains concerned about the ongoing work of the church and writes to Timothy to encourage him in his work.

**Contents**  I. Introduction and greeting (1:1–2)
II. Exhortations on character and spiritual needs (1:3–2:13)
III. Instructions concerning Timothy's work (2:14–4:5)
IV. Epilogue (4:6–22)

# TITUS

**Author**  The apostle Paul, possibly by dictation to another. As with I and II Timothy, there is some question as to the authorship.

**Date of Writing**  A.D. 64 or 65.

**Purpose**  The third of the three "pastoral" epistles (which also include I and II Timothy), The Letter to Titus is written to provide instruction regarding the qualifications and proper behavior of the officers and members of the church.

**Setting**  Titus was a companion of Paul who is referred to in II Corinthians 7:13–15; 8:6, 16, 23. From The Letter to Titus, we learn that Titus was appointed to oversee the church in Crete. We assume that in being asked to prepare to leave (ch. 3:12), Titus was still in Crete when this letter was written. Like I Timothy, Titus was probably written during the years of freedom between Paul's Roman imprisonments.

**Contents**  I. Salutation (1:1–4)

    II. Instructions to Titus (1:5–3:11)

        A. On the qualifications of ministers

        B. On the behavior of people within the church

        C. On the behavior of the church in the world

    III. Personal greetings (3:12–15)

# PHILEMON

**Author** The apostle Paul.

**Date of Writing** A.D. 62 or 63, while Paul was imprisoned in Rome.

**Purpose** To persuade Philemon, a Christian who lived in Colossae, to take back his runaway slave Onesimus, and to treat him with the love becoming his faith.

**Setting** Onesimus, the slave, has run away from his master, Philemon. Somehow Onesimus reaches Paul at Rome. That he has been helpful to Paul is evident from this letter (v. 11), but Paul sends him back, asking Philemon to receive him with love. Another Christian named Tychicus (Col. 4:7–9) accompanies Onesimus with the letter.

**Contents** Only one chapter in length, The Letter to Philemon is a masterpiece of the expression of the nature of the love that must be at the base of all Christian relationships. Paul notes that even though he could order Philemon to take back Onesimus, he would not do that; instead it is seen to be imperative that the two estranged Christians become as brothers. "Receive him as you would receive me," says Paul.

The book may be outlined as follows:

    I. Greetings (vs. 1–3)

    II. Philemon's love and faith recalled (vs. 4–7)

    III. Paul's appeal on behalf of the converted slave (vs. 8–22)

    IV. Closing remarks (vs. 23–25)

# HEBREWS

**Author**   Unknown. The author is a friend of Timothy (13:23–25); thus he is in the Pauline circle.

**Date of Writing**   While Hebrews may have been written in A.D. 65, the more probable date is around A.D. 85. Possibly written from Rome, it is addressed to a group of Jewish Christians.

**Purpose**   To proclaim that Jesus Christ is the final, perfect, and eternal sacrifice, made once for all to atone for the sins of all who believe in him.

**Setting**   Addressed to a Jewish community steeped in the knowledge and history of the worship in the Tabernacle, this letter builds on those old traditions. Referring to the ritual sacrifice made by the High Priest, the author argues that Christ's sacrifice of himself is of infinitely greater worth. He calls Christ a high priest "after the order of Melchizedek"; he notes Christ's flawless credentials and shows how Christ's own shed blood has an infinite capacity to atone for men's sins. This he contrasts to the temporal effect of animal sacrifice. He concludes his argument with a moving exhortation on faith, urging his readers to live boldly in faith, trusting in the salvation that Christ has already obtained for them.

**Contents**   I. God's revelation through his Son (1:1–2:4)
  II. Our redemption through God's Son (2:5–4:13)
     A. Jesus, the pioneer of faith
     B. The Son superior to Moses
  III. Our reconciliation through God's Son (4:14–10:18)
     A. Jesus the great High Priest
     B. Christ's ministry in a heavenly sanctuary
  IV. An exhortation to faith (10:19–13:25)
     A. The faith of men and women of history
     B. A call to run the race with faith

# JAMES

**Author**   Traditionally this letter is assigned to James, the brother of
Jesus, but there are serious questions as to the authorship.

**Date of Writing**   Uncertain. If written by James, the letter may be
dated as early as A.D. 45, when Christians were not yet addressed
as the church, or as late as A.D. 60, for the writer seems aware of
Pauline theology. If, however, this letter was written by another,
as the language and content suggest, it was likely written nearer
the end of the first century.

**Purpose**   To call persons to a singleness of purpose in serving the Lord.

**Setting**   "To the twelve tribes in the Dispersion" may refer to the Jews
scattered across the Mediterranean world, or it may be an address
to the scattered New Israel, the church. At any rate, it is assumed
that the readers have some knowledge of the Jewish background
of the Christian faith, and thus the letter was possibly written at a
time when the church was still primarily Jewish. Since 2:14–26
seems to imply a knowledge of Paul's arguments for justification by
faith, some have argued that James wrote this letter to stop those
who were trying to twist Paul's theology into a do-nothing kind of
faith.

**Contents**   I. The trials that test the faith (1:1–18)
II. "Doers of the word" (1:19–2:26)
III. The Christian temper (3)
IV. Overcoming pride (4)
V. The power of prayer (5)

# I PETER

**Author**   There is some dispute as to the actual author of this letter. The apostle Peter is named as author in 1:1.

**Date of Writing**   If Peter himself was the author of this letter, its date would likely be several years before his death in A.D. 68(?)—perhaps A.D. 65. If, however, it was written by someone else, and if the persecution referred to was that inflicted by the Roman emperor Diocletian, the date would be around A.D. 96.

**Purpose**   To call upon Christians to bear suffering with patience, and with unwavering faith in Christ.

**Setting**   This letter is addressed to the scattered Christians in Asia Minor. The author is in Rome, where persecutions have occurred under Nero. Sensing that the same kind of persecution may spread across the Empire, Peter writes to exhort those in the church to stand firm in the faith.

**Contents**   I. Opening address (1:1–2)
II. Thanksgiving and a call to hope (1:3–25)
III. A call to God's chosen people to right living (2:1–3:7)
IV. How to face persecution and suffering (3:8–4:19)
V. Advice to congregations (5)

# II PETER

**Author**   "Simon Peter" is named in 1:1 as author, but the actual author is unknown.

**Date of Writing**   If Peter wrote this letter, the probable date would be A.D. 67, shortly before Peter's death in Rome. Yet the letter is chiefly concerned with the Gnostic heresy (the teaching that a secret, superior "knowledge" was necessary to be a Christian), which flowered much later. This supports the viewpoint that a much later author (perhaps between A.D. 100 and 125) borrowed Peter's name and attached it to this letter (see below).

**Purpose**   To combat Gnosticism (from *gnōsis*, "knowledge") and call Christians to the true knowledge, which comes only through Jesus Christ.

**Setting**   The Gnostic controversy raged within the church for more than a century. (Gnosticism's secrecy was an attraction; central in its teaching was the notion that all things physical were inferior to things spiritual, and that therefore Christ's physical, earthly life was of little or no importance, compared with his spiritual self.) From 3:15–16 it is clear also that Paul's letters were already widely known in the church when II Peter was written. Furthermore, through the first three centuries, the churches generally refused to accept II Peter as a genuine letter of Peter. All of this indicates that the letter was probably written early in the second century A.D. by an unknown author.

**Contents**   I. A reminder of the basics of the faith (1)
II. Judgment for false preachers (2)
III. Warnings to await Christ's Second Coming (3)

# I JOHN

**Author**  Unnamed; probably John the apostle, author of the Fourth Gospel. A common literary style appears in both the Gospel of John and the first letter of John, as well as in II and III John. If all four are the work of the same author, then either the tradition of John's martyrdom in A.D. 70 is incorrect and he lived to old age—as Irenaeus says—or the author is someone other than John the apostle.

The subject matter of the letters points to a late date for their composition, but internal evidence within the Gospel of John suggests an early date; it also points to John the apostle as the author. While none of the four name him as author, their similarity of style cannot be ignored: if the apostle wrote the Gospel, it is likely that he also wrote the letters. Tradition has long held this to be so, and that would accordingly fix the date of their writing at between A.D. 90 and 100.

**Date of Writing**  Possibly around A.D. 95.

**Purpose**  This book was written to combat the Gnostic heresy (see II Peter) and to call the church to obedience in love.

**Setting**  In its format, I John is not a letter but a sermon. It has no greeting, no salutation, no signature. We do not know the occasion for the writing of this book.

**Contents**  I. The testimony of the gospel (1)
  II. Knowledge of God and resulting love (2:1–17)
  III. The antichrist (2:18–3:3)
  IV. The test of truth and love (3:4–4:21)
  V. Jesus Christ the Son of God (5)

# II JOHN

**Author**   A certain "elder" named John; probably the author of the
Fourth Gospel. But see I John, "Author."
**Date of Writing**   Around A.D. 95.
**Purpose**   This short letter is an exhortation to stand fast in the truth.
**Setting**   Addressed to "the elect lady and her children (probably refer-
ring to members of her church)," this letter amplifies I John's insis-
tence that the one commandment of Christians is to love. The
writer urges his reader to avoid being deceived by any other doc-
trine.
**Contents**   Only 13 verses long, this letter may be outlined as follows:
    I. Greeting
   II. The commandment to love
  III. The importance of avoiding false doctrine
  IV. Personal regards


# III JOHN

**Author**   A certain "elder" named John; probably the author of the
Fourth Gospel. But see I John, "Author."
**Date of Writing**   Perhaps A.D. 96.
**Purpose**   To commend Gaius in his work, particularly in ministry to
strangers.
**Setting**   This is a letter addressed to Gaius, whom the writer calls "be-
loved." He is mentioned nowhere else. Following his commenda-
tion of Gaius, John refers to a certain Diotrephes, who is evidently
troubling the church. We know nothing else of the church of which
they were members.
**Contents**   I. Salutation
   II. Praise for the helpfulness of Gaius
  III. A call to support missionaries
  IV. The troublesome Diotrephes
   V. Exhortation to imitate what is good
  VI. Greetings

# JUDE

**Author**   Jude, who calls himself a brother of James (v. 1), and thereby a brother of Jesus himself (see Mark 6:3).

**Date of Writing**   Since vs. 3 and 17 suggest that this letter was written at a time when the apostles were no longer active, the date of writing would be late, sometime after A.D. 90. The fact that the letter deals with a late first-century heresy makes this date all the more probable.

**Purpose**   To combat Docetism, a heresy that denied the real humanity of Christ. If one supposes that Christ, while on earth, was only a spirit, then logically it is but a step further to deny the importance of physical matter and to say that God is concerned only with things spiritual. And if only the spiritual is important, then—according to Docetism—it does not matter what Christians do with their bodies as they live out their physical lives. (Also see II Peter, concerning Gnosticism.)

**Setting**   Jude had apparently learned that those who followed this new heresy had gained membership within the church itself, teaching that God's grace allows persons to live as they please. This letter is a sharp rebuke to such doctrine. It is addressed to all Christians: "To those who are called."

**Contents**   I. Greeting
II. Grace is being perverted into licentiousness
III. Warning of God's judgment
IV. Exhortation to faithfulness
V. Ascription of praise to God

# REVELATION

**Author**   A certain John. Although The Revelation to John is traditionally attributed to the author of the Fourth Gospel, great differences
in style make this identification unlikely.

**Date of Writing**   About A.D. 96.

**Purpose**   To reveal, through a series of visions, the future triumph of
God over the forces of evil. The word "revelation" is, in the Greek,
"apocalypse," which means, literally, "an uncovering" (see on Daniel). The book is sometimes called by its Greek name, The Apocalypse.

**Setting**   During the reign of Domitian (A.D. 81–96), Rome began a
systematic campaign to make the worship of the emperor the only
religion permitted within the Empire. A reign of terror followed,
and Christians were forced to choose between renouncing their
Lord or facing torture and death. In the midst of this situation John
was banished to the island of Patmos, where God showed him a
series of terrible visions, culminating with the final victory of Christ
and the rise of a new Jerusalem. He describes those visions in this
book, which he addresses "to the seven churches that are in Asia."

**Contents**   I. Introductions and greetings (1:1–8)
   II. The visions (1:9–22:5)
      A. The church on earth (1:9–3:22)
      B. The Lamb and the scroll (4:1–8:1)
      C. The trumpets (8:2–11:19)
      D. The church persecuted (12:1–14:20)
      E. The bowls of judgment (15–16)
      F. Babylon's judgment (17:1–19:10)
      G. Victory and the new Jerusalem (19:11–22:5)
   III. The testimony of John (22:6–21)

# Westminster Historical Maps of Bible Lands

EDITED BY

## G. ERNEST WRIGHT

## FLOYD V. FILSON

## HOW TO USE THE MAPS

WE NEED ONLY TO CONSIDER how the face of Europe has changed since World War I, or how the Western Hemisphere has developed since the days of Columbus, in order to see just how much the ancient world could and did change between the years 2000 B.C. and A.D. 100.

The Westminster Historical Maps of Bible Lands on the pages that follow present an accurate picture of both Palestine and the larger ancient world at different points in their past.

It is important that the reader utilize a map depicting the world as it existed at the time of the Biblical passage being studied. For example, to trace the events described in Genesis 21–50, the reader should consult Plate II, which gives a wide picture of the world between 2000 and 1700 B.C. Or, to see how the Promised Land was apportioned among the twelve tribes following the conquest of Canaan, turn to Plate IV, which shows Palestine as it looked during the years between 1225 and 1025 B.C. Plate XIV reveals the numerous political changes that had occurred in that same area by the time of Christ.

Plate I is an excellent representation of the physical features of Palestine, and any student of the Bible will do well to examine that map in detail at the outset in order to become familiar with the unchanging topography of the Holy Land.

The maps are arranged chronologically, from the earliest to the latest Biblical times.

Also included is a detailed index to the maps, providing a means of quickly locating practically any place mentioned in the Bible.

By using these maps in conjunction with the chronologies, the reader will soon acquire such a sense of Biblical history as to hear and understand with a remarkable new clarity the Word that God has spoken across the centuries.

# TABLE OF MAPS

# MAP INDEX

PLATE I

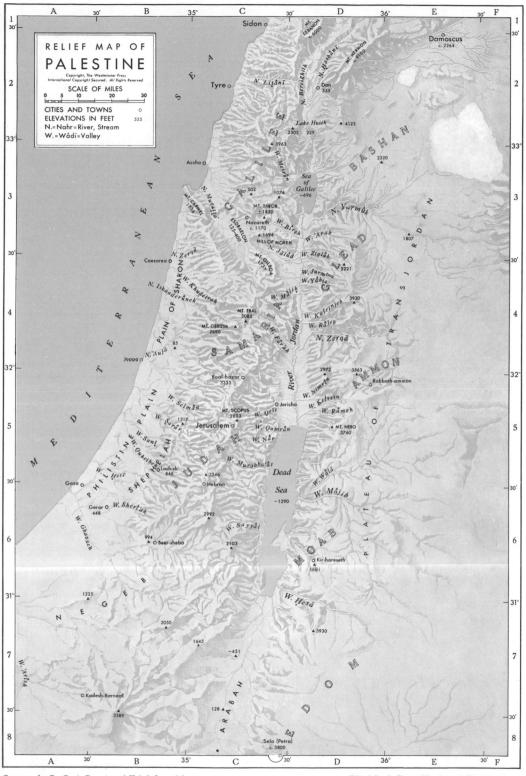

RELIEF MAP OF
# PALESTINE
SCALE OF MILES

0    5    10         20         30

CITIES AND TOWNS          o
ELEVATIONS IN FEET        555
N.=Nahr=River, Stream
W.=Wâdī=Valley

Sidon

MT. LEBANON c. 6000

Damascus c. 2264

N. Berdâhila

N. Hasbânī

MT. HERMON 9100

Tyre

N. Liṭânī

Dan 555

M E D I T E R R A N E A N   S E A

Lake Huleh 2303   229   ▲ 4123

2320

N. Meîrôn   ▲ 3963

B A S H A N

Accho o

MT. CARMEL 1726

G A L I L E E

▲ 502   ▲ 1074

Sea of Galilee -696

N. Yurmûk

MT. TABOR ±1850

W. Bîreh

1807

Caesarea o

N. Zerqâ

Nazareth c. 1170

ESDRAELON 125-400

W. 'Arab

MT. GILBOA 1737   ▲ 1694

HILL OF MOREH

W. Ziqlâb

N. Jalûd

W. Jurm

W. Yâbis   ▲ 2221

N. Iskanderûneh

W. Khuderrah

P L A I N   O F   S H A R O N

MT. EBAL 3085

W. Mâlih

J o r d a n

G I L E A D

W. Kufrinjeh   ▲ 3930

N. Zerqâ

MT. GERIZIM 2890

W. Fâr'ah

N. 'Aujâ   ▲ 85

Joppa o

S A M A R I A

R i v e r

T R A N S J O R D A N

Baal-hazor 3333

▲ 2972   ▲ 3563

A M M O N

Rabbath-ammon

W. Selmân

W. Nimrîn

W. Sarâr

MT. SCOPUS 2693

o Jericho

W. Kefrein

1317

Jerusalem

W. Qelt

W. Râmeh

P L A I N

W. Sant

W. Qumrân

▲ MT. NEBO 3760

P H I L I S T I N E

W. Osteibeh

W. Nâr

S H E P H E L A H

Lachish o 846

W. Murabba'ât

J U D A H

Gaza o

Hesî

▲ 3346

o Hebron

Dead Sea -1290

W. Wâlâ

Gerar o 448

W. Shert'ah

▲ 2992

W. Môjib

994

o Beer-sheba

W. Sayyâl

▲ 2103

M O A B

W. Ghazzeh

Kir-hareseth

N E G E B

▲ 1225

W. Hesâ

2050

▲ 3930

1645

▲ -451

W. 'Arîsa

E D O M

o Kadesh-Barnea?

A R A B A H

128

▲ 3389

Sela (Petra) c. 3800

Cartography By G. A. Barrois and Hal & Jean Arbo          Edited By G. Ernest Wright and Floyd V. Filson

PLATE II

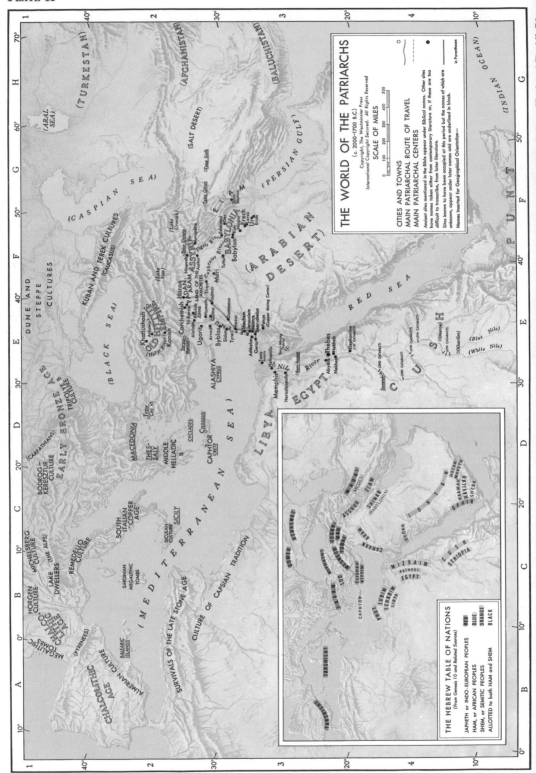

THE WORLD OF THE PATRIARCHS
(c. 2000–1700 B.C.)

Copyright, The Westminster Press
International Copyright Secured. All Rights Reserved

SCALE OF MILES

CITIES AND TOWNS
MAIN PATRIARCHAL ROUTE OF TRAVEL
MAIN PATRIARCHAL CENTERS

Ancient sites mentioned in the Bible appear under Biblical names. Other sites have names taken either from contemporary literature or, if these are too difficult to translate, from later literature.

Sites known to have been occupied at this period but the names of which are unknown, appear under later names odd are underlined in block.

Names inserted for Geographical Orientation—

in Parentheses

THE HEBREW TABLE OF NATIONS
(from Genesis 10 and Related Sources)

JAPHETH or INDO-EUROPEAN PEOPLES — RED
HAM, or AFRICAN PEOPLES — BLUE
SHEM, or SEMITIC PEOPLES — ORANGE
ALLOTTED to both HAM and SHEM — BLACK

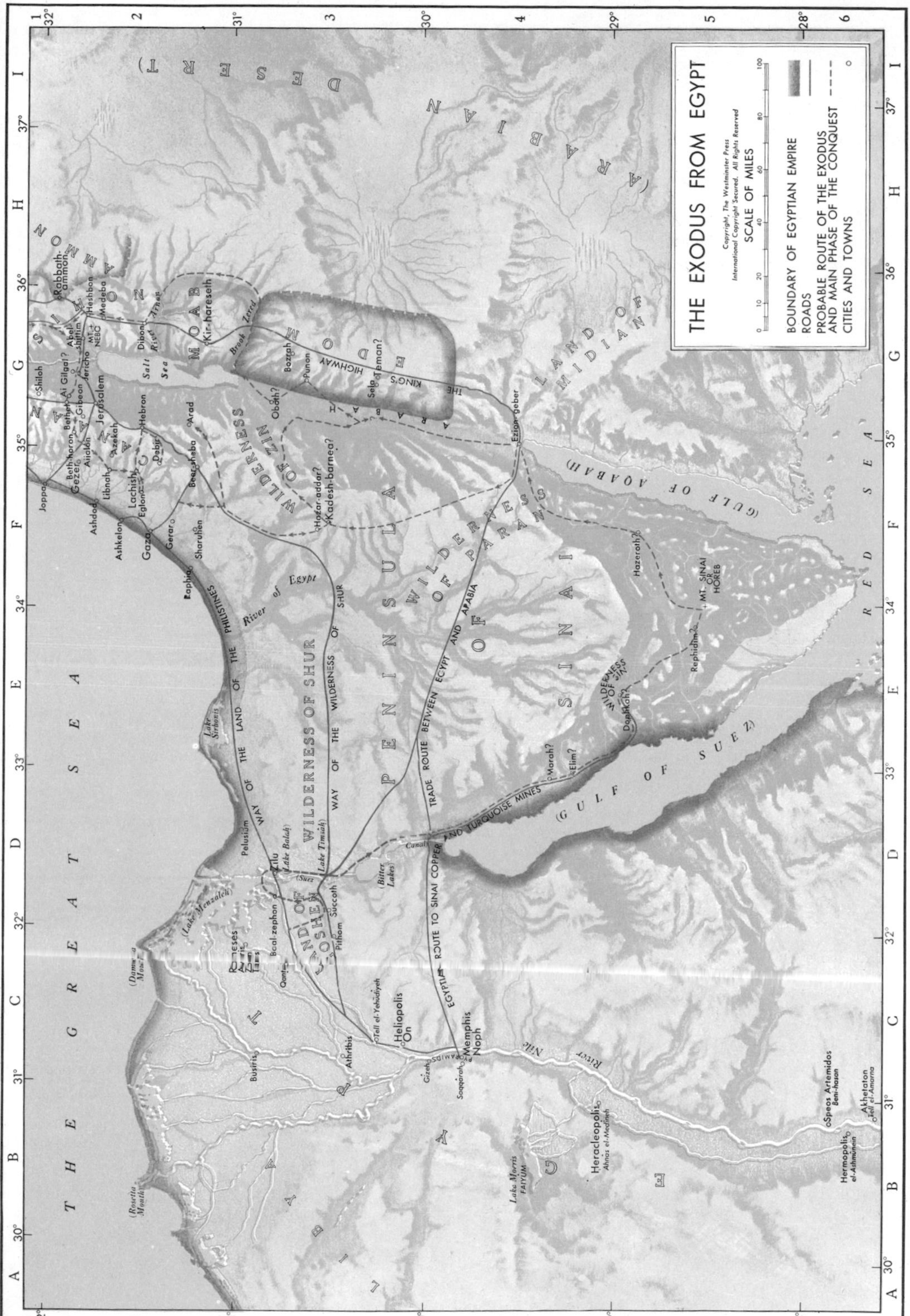

PLATE III

THE EXODUS FROM EGYPT

SCALE OF MILES

0   10   20        40        60        80        100

BOUNDARY OF EGYPTIAN EMPIRE

ROADS

PROBABLE ROUTE OF THE EXODUS
AND MAIN PHASE OF THE CONQUEST

CITIES AND TOWNS

Edited By G. Ernest Wright and Floyd V. Filson

Cartography By Hal & Jean Arbo

PLATE IV

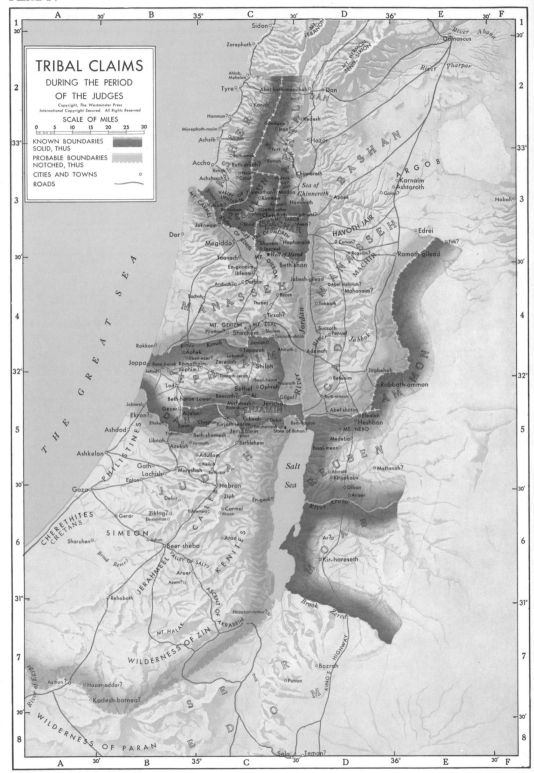

TRIBAL CLAIMS
DURING THE PERIOD
OF THE JUDGES

SCALE OF MILES

0   5   10   15   20   25   30

KNOWN BOUNDARIES
SOLID, THUS

PROBABLE BOUNDARIES
NOTCHED, THUS

CITIES AND TOWNS

ROADS

*Cartography By G. A. Barrois and Hal & Jean Arbo*        *Edited By G. Ernest Wright and Floyd V. Filson*

PLATE V

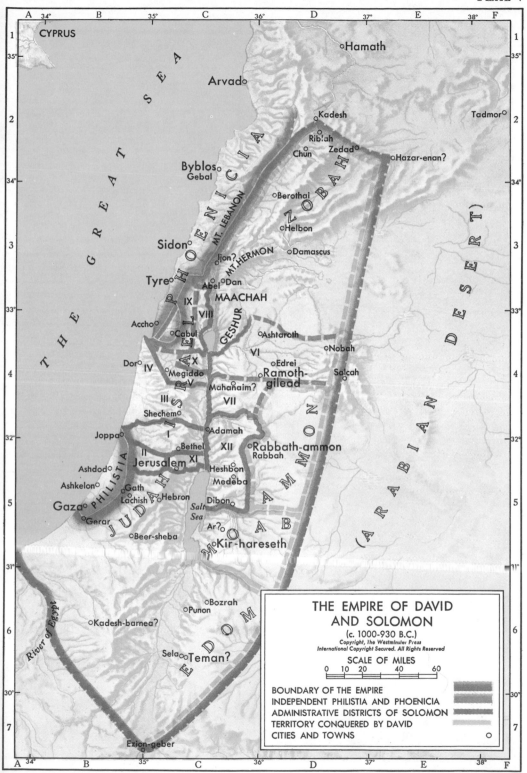

THE EMPIRE OF DAVID
AND SOLOMON
(c. 1000-930 B.C.)
Copyright, The Westminster Press
International Copyright Secured. All Rights Reserved

SCALE OF MILES
0  10  20        40         60

BOUNDARY OF THE EMPIRE
INDEPENDENT PHILISTIA AND PHOENICIA
ADMINISTRATIVE DISTRICTS OF SOLOMON
TERRITORY CONQUERED BY DAVID
CITIES AND TOWNS

CYPRUS
Hamath
Arvad
THE GREAT SEA
Kadesh
Tadmor
Riblah
Zedad
Chun
Hazar-enan?
Byblos
Gebal
PHOENICIA
MT. LEBANON
ZOBAH
Berothai
Helbon
Sidon
Jion?
MT. HERMON
Damascus
Tyre
Abel Dan
(ARABIAN DESERT)
IX
MAACHAH
Accho
VIII
GESHUR
Ashtaroth
Cabul
VI
Nobah
Dor
IV
X
Edrei
Salcah
Megiddo
Ramoth-
gilead
V
Mahanaim?
ISRAEL
III
VII
AMMON
Shechem
Joppa
I
Adamah
Bethel
XII
Rabbath-ammon
II
Jerusalem
XI
Rabbah
Ashdod
Heshbon
Ashkelon
Gath
Medeba
Lachish
Gaza
Hebron
Dibon
PHILISTIA
JUDAH
Salt
Sea
MOAB
Gerar
Ar?
Beer-sheba
Kir-hareseth
River of Egypt
Bozrah
Punon
EDOM
Kadesh-barnea?
Sela
Teman?
Ezion-geber

Cartography By Hal & Jean Arbo                    Edited By G. Ernest Wright and Floyd V. Filson

PLATE VI

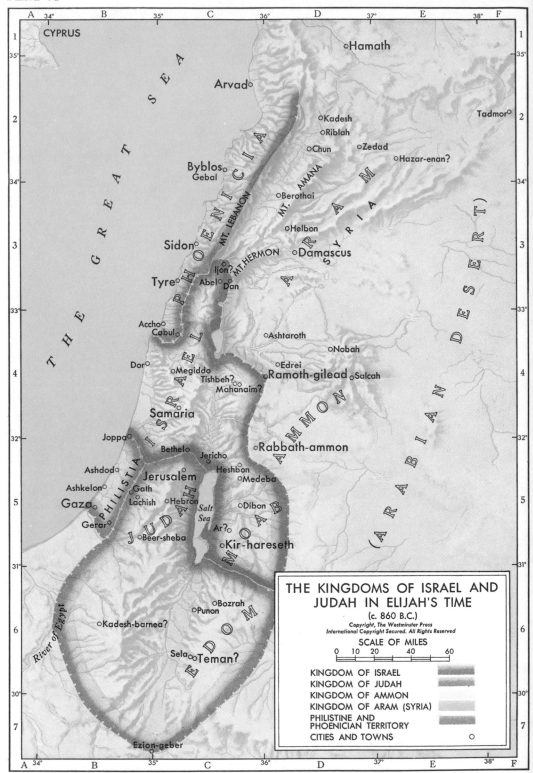

THE KINGDOMS OF ISRAEL AND
JUDAH IN ELIJAH'S TIME
(c. 860 B.C.)

Copyright, The Westminster Press
International Copyright Secured. All Rights Reserved

SCALE OF MILES

0    10   20      40        60

KINGDOM OF ISRAEL
KINGDOM OF JUDAH
KINGDOM OF AMMON
KINGDOM OF ARAM (SYRIA)
PHILISTINE AND
PHOENICIAN TERRITORY
CITIES AND TOWNS          ○

*Cartography By Hal & Jean Arbo*          *Edited By G. Ernest Wright and Floyd V. Filson*

PLATE VII

THE KINGDOM OF JUDAH
IN ISAIAH'S TIME
(c. 700 B.C.)
Copyright, The Westminster Press
International Copyright Secured. All Rights Reserved

SCALE OF MILES
0  10  20      40      60

ASSYRIAN EMPIRE
KINGDOM OF JUDAH
KINGDOM OF EDOM
KINGDOM OF MOAB
KINGDOM OF AMMON
INDEPENDENT TYRE          *
ASSYRIAN PROVINCES    DU'RU
CITIES AND TOWNS          o

*Cartography By Hal & Jean Arbo*

*Edited By G. Ernest Wright and Floyd V. Filson*

PLATE VIII

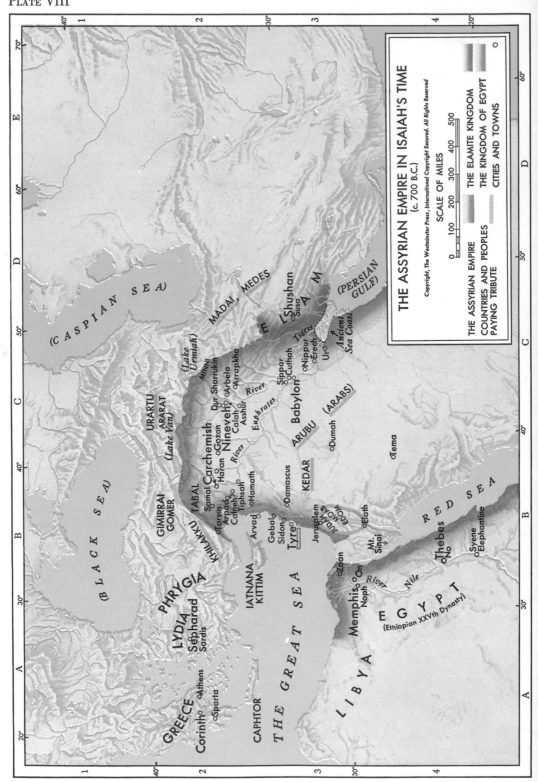

THE ASSYRIAN EMPIRE IN ISAIAH'S TIME
(c. 700 B.C.)

Copyright, The Westminster Press, International Copyright Secured, All Rights Reserved

SCALE OF MILES

0   100   200   300   400   500

THE ASSYRIAN EMPIRE

COUNTRIES AND PEOPLES

PAYING TRIBUTE

THE ELAMITE KINGDOM

THE KINGDOM OF EGYPT

CITIES AND TOWNS

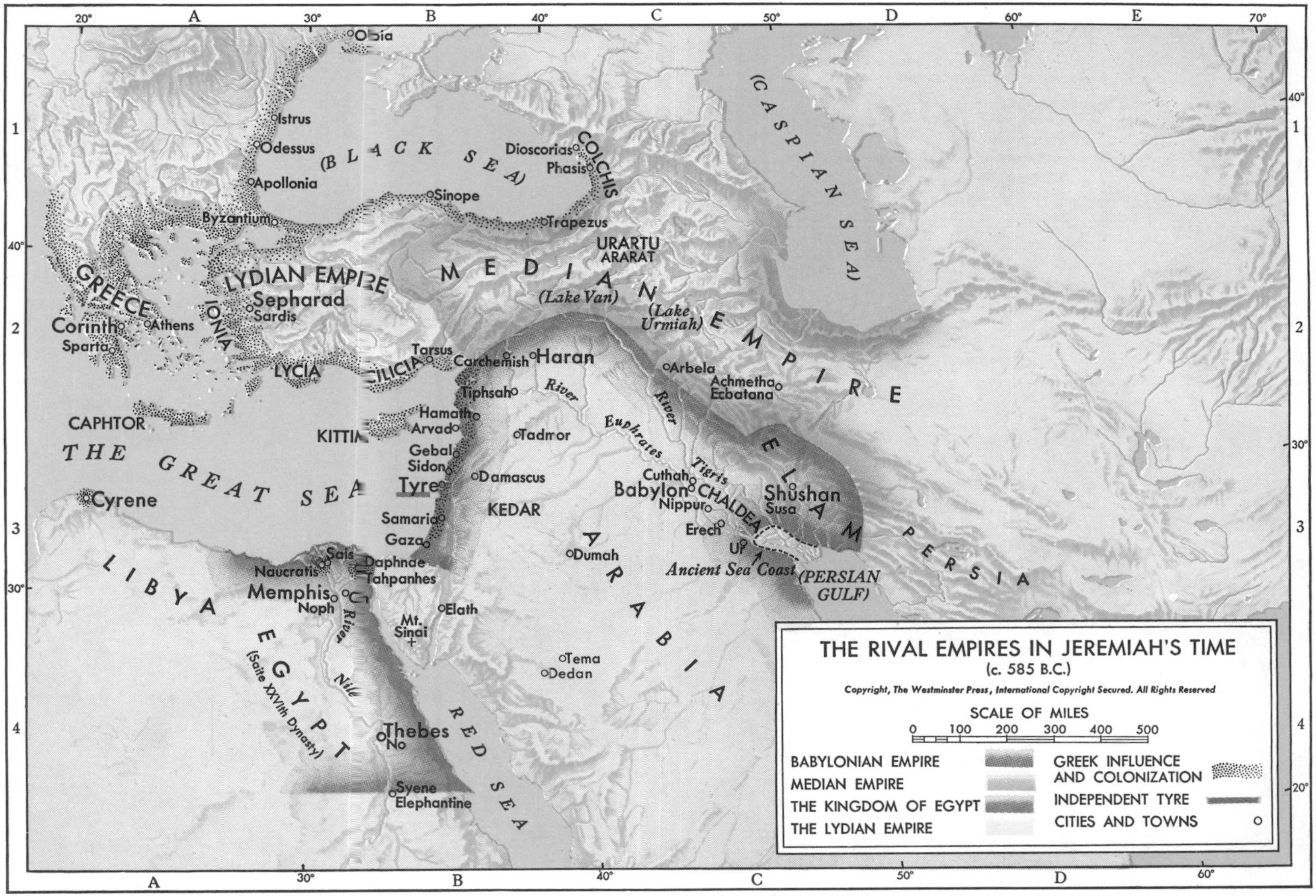

PLATE IX

THE RIVAL EMPIRES IN JEREMIAH'S TIME
(c. 585 B.C.)

Copyright, The Westminster Press, International Copyright Secured. All Rights Reserved

SCALE OF MILES

0   100   200   300   400   500

BABYLONIAN EMPIRE
MEDIAN EMPIRE
THE KINGDOM OF EGYPT
THE LYDIAN EMPIRE

GREEK INFLUENCE
AND COLONIZATION
INDEPENDENT TYRE
CITIES AND TOWNS

Edited By G. Ernest Wright and Floyd V. Filson

Cartography By Hal & Jean Arbo

PLATE X

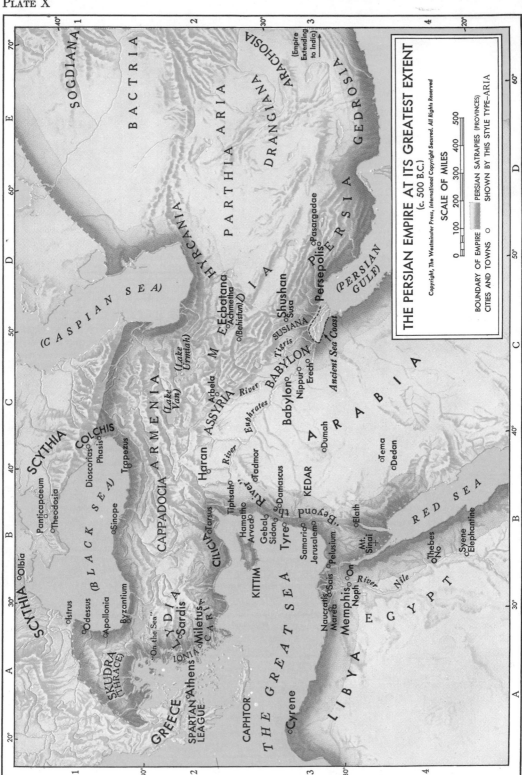

THE PERSIAN EMPIRE AT ITS GREATEST EXTENT

(c. 500 B.C.)

SCALE OF MILES

0   100   200   300   400   500

BOUNDARY OF EMPIRE
CITIES AND TOWNS ○

PERSIAN SATRAPIES (PROVINCES)
SHOWN BY THIS STYLE TYPE—ARIA

Edited By C. Ernest Wright and Floyd V. Filson

Cartography By Hal & Jean Ashe

PLATE XI

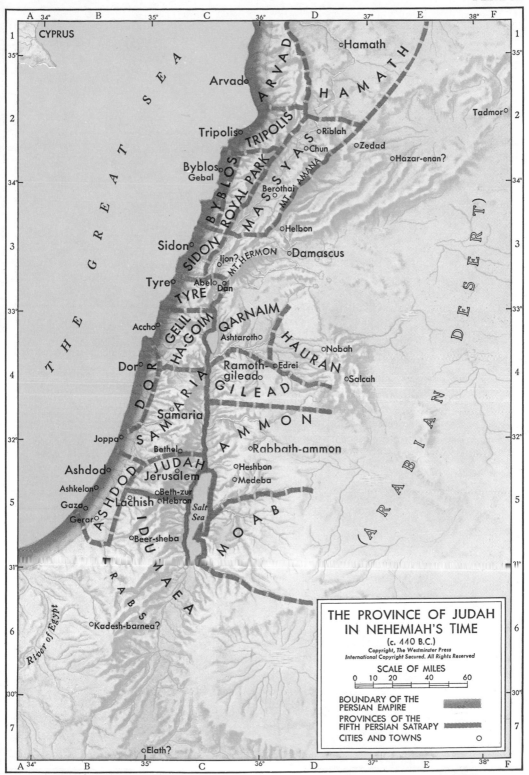

CYPRUS

THE GREAT SEA

Arvado
ARVAD
Hamath
HAMATH
Tadmor

Tripolis
TRIPOLIS
Riblah
Chun
Zedad
Hazar-enan?

Byblos
Gebal
BYBLOS
ROYAL PARK
MASSYAS
Berothai
MT. AMANA
Helbon

Sidon
SIDON
Ijon?
MT. HERMON
Damascus

Tyre
TYRE
Abelo
Dan
QARNAIM
Ashtaroth
HAURAN
Nobah

Accho
GELIL
HA-GOIM
Ramoth-gilead
Edrei
Salcah

Dor
DOR
GILEAD

Samaria
SAMARIA
AMMON

Joppa
Bethel
Rabbath-ammon

Ashdod
ASHDOD
JUDAH
Jerusalem
Heshbon
Medeba

Ashkelon
Beth-zur
Hebron

Gaza
Lachish
Salt Sea

Gerar
IDUMAEA
Beer-sheba
MOAB

ARABS

River of Egypt

Kadesh-barnea?

(ARABIAN DESERT)

Elath?

### THE PROVINCE OF JUDAH
### IN NEHEMIAH'S TIME
#### (c. 440 B.C.)

SCALE OF MILES

0  10  20      40      60

BOUNDARY OF THE
PERSIAN EMPIRE

PROVINCES OF THE
FIFTH PERSIAN SATRAPY

CITIES AND TOWNS            o

Cartography By Hal & Jean Arbo

Edited By G. Ernest Wright and Floyd V. Filson

PLATE XII

PALESTINE
IN THE
MACCABEAN PERIOD
(168-63 B.C.)

Copyright, The Westminster Press
International Copyright Secured. All Rights Reserved

SCALE OF MILES

0    5   10        20        30

BOUNDARY LINE SHOWS MAXIMUM
EXTENT OF MACCABEAN KINGDOM
UNDER ALEXANDER JANNAEUS
(103-76 B.C.)

KINGDOM OF
ALEXANDER JANNAEUS

FREE CITY

CITIES AND TOWNS        ○

Cartography By G. A. Barrois and Hal & Jean Arbo

Edited By G. Ernest Wright and Floyd V. Filson

PLATE XIII

PALESTINE
UNDER
HEROD THE GREAT
(40-4 B.C.)

Copyright, The Westminster Press
International Copyright Secured. All Rights Reserved

SCALE OF MILES

0   5  10      20        30

KINGDOM OF
HEROD THE GREAT

DECAPOLIS

FREE CITY

CITIES AND TOWNS        ○

*Cartography By G. A. Barrois and Hal & Jean Arbo*                    *Edited By G. Ernest Wright and Floyd V. Filson*

Plate XIV

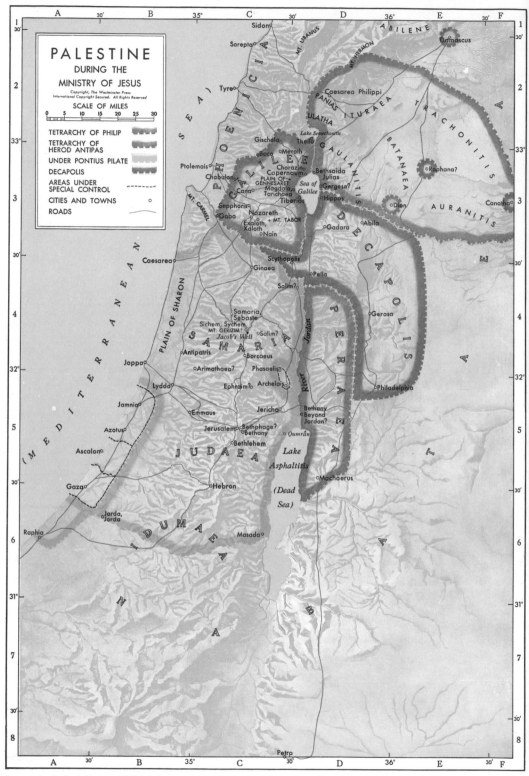

PALESTINE
DURING THE
MINISTRY OF JESUS

Copyright, The Westminster Press
International Copyright Secured. All Rights Reserved

SCALE OF MILES

0   5   10   15   20   25   30

TETRARCHY OF PHILIP
TETRARCHY OF
HEROD ANTIPAS
UNDER PONTIUS PILATE
DECAPOLIS
AREAS UNDER
SPECIAL CONTROL
CITIES AND TOWNS          o
ROADS

*Cartography By G. A. Barrois and Hal & Jean Arbo*          *Edited By G. Ernest Wright and Floyd V. Filson*

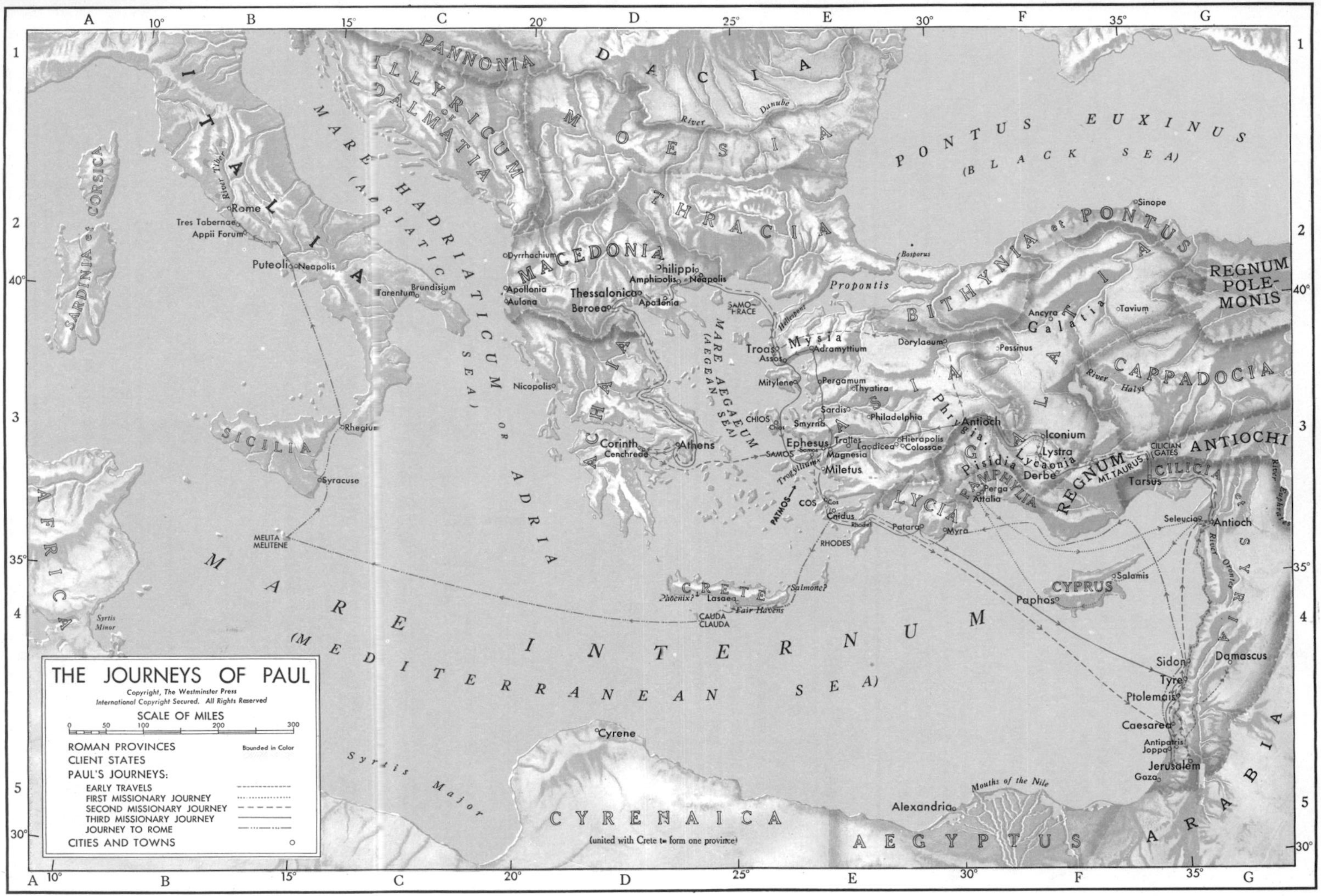

PLATE XV

Edited By G. Ernest Wright and Floyd V. Filson

Cartography By Hal & Jean Arbo

THE JOURNEYS OF PAUL

Copyright, The Westminster Press
International Copyright Secured. All Rights Reserved

SCALE OF MILES

ROMAN PROVINCES
CLIENT STATES
Bounded in Color

PAUL'S JOURNEYS:
EARLY TRAVELS
FIRST MISSIONARY JOURNEY
SECOND MISSIONARY JOURNEY
THIRD MISSIONARY JOURNEY
JOURNEY TO ROME
CITIES AND TOWNS

PLATE XVI

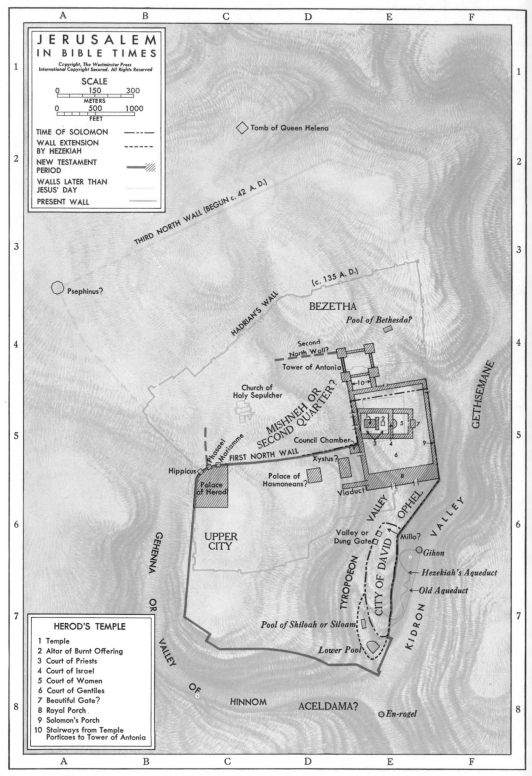

JERUSALEM
IN BIBLE TIMES

Copyright, The Westminster Press
International Copyright Secured. All Rights Reserved

SCALE

0    150    300
METERS
0    500    1000
FEET

TIME OF SOLOMON        — · — · —
WALL EXTENSION         — — — —
BY HEZEKIAH
NEW TESTAMENT
PERIOD
WALLS LATER THAN
JESUS' DAY
PRESENT WALL

◇ Tomb of Queen Helena

THIRD NORTH WALL (BEGUN c. 42 A. D.)

(c. 135 A. D.)

⬡ Psephinus?

HADRIAN'S WALL

BEZETHA

Pool of Bethesda?

Second
North Wall?

Tower of Antonia

Church of
Holy Sepulcher

MISHNEH OR
SECOND QUARTER?

Phasael
Mariamme

Hippicus

FIRST NORTH WALL

Council Chamber

Xystus?

GETHSEMANE

Palace
of Herod

Palace of
Hasmoneans?

Viaduct

UPPER
CITY

GEHENNA

OR

VALLEY

OF

HINNOM

TYROPOEON

VALLEY

OPHEL

Valley or
Dung Gate

Millo?

CITY OF DAVID

◇ Gihon

← Hezekiah's Aqueduct

← Old Aqueduct

KIDRON

VALLEY

Pool of Shiloah or Siloam

Lower Pool

ACELDAMA?

◇ En-rogel

HEROD'S TEMPLE

1 Temple
2 Altar of Burnt Offering
3 Court of Priests
4 Court of Israel
5 Court of Women
6 Court of Gentiles
7 Beautiful Gate?
8 Royal Porch
9 Solomon's Porch
10 Stairways from Temple
   Porticoes to Tower of Antonia

Cartography By Hal & Jean Arbo

Edited By G. Ernest Wright and Floyd V. Filson